THE COST
OF CARING

Wiley Personal Finance Solutions

THE COST OF CARING

Money Skills for Caregivers

ANNE M. JOHNSON
RUTH REJNIS

JOHN WILEY & SONS, INC.

New York • Chichester • Weinheim • Brisbane • Singapore • Toronto

This book is printed on acid-free paper. ∞

Copyright © 1998 by Anne M. Johnson and Ruth Rejnis. All rights reserved.
Published by John Wiley & Sons, Inc.

Published simultaneously in Canada.

This publication is designed to provide accurate and authoritative information in
regard to the subject matter covered. It is sold with the understanding that the pub-
lisher is not engaged in rendering professional services. If professional advice or
other expert assistance is required, the services of a competent professional person
should be sought.

Library of Congress Cataloging-in-Publication Data:

Johnson, Anne M., 1948-
    The cost of caring : money skills for caregivers / by Anne M.
  Johnson and Ruth Rejnis.
      p. cm.
    Includes index.
    ISBN 0-471-23925-9 (pbk. : alk. paper)
      1. Caregivers—Finance, Personal.   2. Finance, Personal.
  I. Rejnis, Ruth.   II. Title.
  HG179.J542   1998
  332.024—dc21   98-16191

Printed in the United States of America.

10 9 8 7 6 5 4 3 2 1

CONTENTS

$

ACKNOWLEDGMENTS

Our appreciation to the many caregivers who so generously shared their time, experiences, and suggestions with us.

And with special thanks for their assistance to Rebecca L. Berg, Esq., S. Gardner Riel, and Carolyn Janik.

Part One

THE PERSONAL SIDE OF CAREGIVING

This book is, of course, about dollars and cents. Over the next 20 chapters, you will read a good deal about finances as they apply to caregiving.

Part 1, however, focuses on the *care* part of that word. Although you will certainly find suggestions for the family surrounding the care recipient, most of the information in the next six chapters is directed at you in your role as caregiver and how you can make that situation as workable and efficient as possible, while still being a loving and compassionate family member or friend to your care recipient. There's some money talk, naturally, with suggestions and exercises that could affect your present lifestyle, your home, and your job—all positively, at this busy, perhaps worrisome, time for you.

$

You're Really Not Alone

Since the beginning of man's—and woman's—time on earth, caregiving has been a natural part of the human experience. To care for another person, whether that person is a spouse, a parent, a child, another relative, or a friend, is an act of love, and, yes, can even be an act of duty.

In an earlier era, families lived close to one another or even shared households, and the word *caregiving*, as it pertains to families, had not been coined. That's because "caring for your own" was simply what people did; it didn't need a name.

Only in modern times has the word *caregiving* come into popular use. Both medical science and demographics have played roles.

Seniors—along with the rest of us—are living longer than ever. In the past, victims of stroke, heart attack, spinal cord injuries, and various diseases died sooner than they do now because doctors could not draw on the array of technology and the body of research they can today. Think about it: Organ transplants are almost commonplace. A person who has had a heart attack is often home from the hospital within a week. Cancer and other serious diseases can be treated.

And yet, in some instances, although those people who would have died from their illnesses or injuries as recently as 20 years ago may live today, the quality of their lives could well be diminished. Some may need looking after for a few years; others, for the rest of their lives.

Moreover, pressured by rising health care costs, hospitals discharge patients more quickly. They are sent home or to rehabilitation centers, often with an ongoing need for someone to care for them. The help they need may be limited or intense.

As medical science advances, the number of people needing care—and the number of people who must look after them—continues to grow.

Demographics play a large role in the caregiving scene, too. The sheer number of seniors in their 70s, 80s, and, increasingly frequently, 90s is growing. Right behind them are the baby boomers, who represent the post–World War II boom of children now approaching their 40s and 50s.

But the baby boomers are a different breed from their parents, today's seniors. The boomers left home for college and many never returned. When their parents need help, they may not be available because they no longer live close by. Divorce is more commonplace in this group, resulting in extended families that include half siblings, stepchildren, and multiple family units. That further complicates the caregiving picture and sometimes results in severed biological family ties or closer ties to extended family members. Another result of demographic dynamics is that many people feel closer to friends than to family.

A CAREGIVER DEFINITION—PLEASE

The word *caregiver* now applies to anyone who tends to someone he or she loves, regardless of that person's relationship or age, or of the duration and amount of care.

The scope of care provided may range from as little as checking in on someone from time to time to taking full responsibility for the loved one's daily care and financial affairs.

There are two particularly common caregiving situations: an elder caring for an ailing spouse or other relative, and a middle-aged son or daughter looking after an ailing parent, perhaps while raising his or her own family and holding a job as well. The latter have become known as the "sandwich generation": These people's lives are sandwiched between the needs of their parents and those of their children.

Since these two are the caregiving situations with the greatest numbers, this book is directed more to them. If you don't fall into one of these categories, don't stop reading. All caregivers will find information within these pages that they can apply to their own or to a loved one's situation.

▼▼▼

After "To Love," "To Help" is
the most beautiful verb in the world.
Baroness Bertha von Suttner, EPIGRAM

▲▲▲

YOUR FELLOW CAREGIVERS

If you are not alone, then how many caregivers are out there? No one knows for sure, although various estimates put the number at 50 million. That includes part-time as well as full-time caregivers. It includes people who are caregivers for a short period of time—say, to help a parent recover from a heart attack or stroke—as well as those who care for a loved one at home for several years and eventually transfer that person to a nursing home.

Studies on caregivers in the workforce estimate that 15% to 30% of all workers are looking after a loved one in some capacity. Using the full range of those percentages translates to 19 million to 38 million working caregivers, based on the 1990 census of employed Americans.

That's a lot of caregivers, and, as you might expect, there is a huge and growing reservoir of resources to help this group of special people at the national and the grassroots levels.

A RESOURCES EXPLOSION

An entire industry has sprung up around this huge number of caregivers. Ten years ago there were few groups dedicated to caregiver advocacy, few regional magazines, and only a handful of Web sites on the Internet. Today, a half-dozen national and an untold number of regional and local caregiver associations have been formed. Many states and cities have publications dedicated to caregivers, and books for caregivers abound. But the explosion of Internet sites tells the real story: over 3,000 sites aimed at caregivers, where quite recently there were less than 100.

That may pose another problem for caregivers. Faced with so many resources, where do you begin? Who are these groups and associations, what do they do, and how can they help?

Help is available at the national, state, and local levels. At all three levels, resources include government agencies and programs, nonprofit organizations, and for-profit companies. The help they provide includes direct services, such as home care, respite care, or support groups; products, such as medical equipment and personal items; and publications: books, pamphlets, guides, and perhaps even a newspaper or magazine dedicated to caregiving. Let's look at these resources level by level.

HELP IN YOUR COMMUNITY

Most of the hands-on services and support you will need are right there in your community. Residents of large cities and urban areas will probably find a greater number of resources than will those in small towns or rural areas. At the same time, there may be a greater demand for services in large cities.

Tax-poor localities have government resources because funds for federal programs often are allocated to states, which funnel them to local governments and nonprofit agencies to administer where they are needed in a community.

For government-funded programs (you'll read about specific ones throughout this book), start at your community's agency on aging or city department of elder affairs. One or more of these will be listed in the blue or government pages section of your local telephone book.

Nonprofit groups are found in every community. They receive city or county, state, and federal funds to fulfill certain programs.

Nonprofits also fill unmet needs in a community, for which they rely on grants and donations.

Some nonprofits are disease specific, such as Alzheimer's Association chapters; others may address many caregiver issues. If your care recipient has a specific disease, begin your search by looking for an association's local chapter. There you may find assistance for the particular need and information on what else is available.

In addition to providing direct services, organizations in your town may offer emotional, financial, and legal help. Your community probably has periodic free seminars and conferences sponsored by private companies, city government, and nonprofit organizations that will help you even further. While researching local resources, you will find that each one has different things to offer and some may overlap.

During your search, don't overlook relatives, friends, neighbors, and religious organizations.

The key is to ask, ask, ask. No one knows your area better than someone who works or lives there. And each person you talk with usually leads you to another resource. Don't become discouraged at this caregiving maze. Keep asking until you find the answers you need.

HIDDEN RESOURCES

Sometimes resources are not readily apparent; that is, you won't find them listed in a book, or a local agency won't know about them. This happens because they are one-time occurrences. Here's a real-life example. A national durable medical equipment company came out with a new line of equipment. Its local offices had to sell the older model quickly or dispose of it. One local office decided to give the equipment to a nonprofit group for a tax break on the charitable donation. The nonprofit organization gave the equipment to a few of its most needy members.

Let other people know about your situation as well—even doctors. Some pharmaceutical and medical equipment companies provide doctors with drugs or equipment earmarked for patients in need. When these free items become available, your doctor or another individual will think about you—but only if they know about you! Caregiving is a maze. However, lots of people are in that maze to help you through it.

▼ **DID YOU KNOW . . .**
If you can't locate resources on your own, call the Eldercare Locator at (800) 677-1116. This national hot line will refer you to help in your community.

For-profit companies fill in the huge gaps left by government and nonprofit agencies when you or loved ones are unable to qualify or there is a waiting list for services.

As you will learn in upcoming chapters, insurance companies, Medicare, and Medicaid may pay for many of the services or products you might need.

HELP AT STATE AND NATIONAL LEVELS

States' resources are vast. Most states have a department of elder affairs, which can guide you to resources in or near your community or tell you about state-funded programs for caregivers and elders.

Other helpful departments (and each state may have a different name for them) could be those governing insurance, families and children, real estate, medical professionals, hospitals, and nursing homes. These departments usually distribute free publications, and some may have people available to answer questions you may have.

Your state probably has at least one, and maybe several, universities, too. A growing number of colleges and universities have gerontology programs that could provide direct help or refer you to an agency that can. Many universities have research centers focusing on caregiver and senior issues. Free publications and direct services may be available.

There are several groups around the country that you will particularly want to know about. Sometimes that is because they are nationwide and you need the help of a large organization. Sometimes you will find them especially useful to you because they focus on one particular caregiving area. Or you may see them mentioned often in caregiving literature and recognize that it will pay to have their addresses handy for future reference.

You've probably heard of many of them: National Institutes for Health, Department of Labor, Social Security Administration, Agency for Health Care Administration. Adhering to laws passed by Congress, these federal agencies make rules about what programs should be established and who qualifies for them. They dole out the funds that Congress appropriates for national programs.

Among the association names you've probably heard are the American Cancer Society and the Alzheimer's Association. Following are a few more, the most prominent of the caregiving groups and associations operating nationally.

American Association of Retired Persons
601 East St. NW
Washington, DC 20049
(800) 424-3410
www.aarp.org
Though a nonprofit organization for people age 50 and older, the AARP has many caregiving resources, such as a free magazine, pamphlets, and brochures on most every issue concerning seniors, from long-distance caregiving to understanding Medicare. It offers a 24-hour hot line, legal counsel, and much more. The Web site has chat rooms and on-line help. The cost to join is $8 a year.

Caregiver Network
www.caregiver.on.ca
This Toronto, Canada–based organization offers on-line support, chat rooms, referrals, and information.

Caregiver Resource
www.caregiver911.com
This on-line resource site by Jim and Merlene Sherman, authors of the Caregiver Survival Series, provides links to many senior and caregiving resources and information, including books and publications.

Children of Aging Parents
1609 Woodbourne Road, Suite 302A
Levittown, PA 19057-1511
(215) 945-6900 or (800) 227-7294
Provides information on caregiver issues and referrals to local support groups and care managers.

Family Caregivers Alliance
425 Bush St., Suite 500
San Francisco, CA 94108
(415) 434-3388 or (800) 896-3650
www.info@caregiver.org
This nonprofit organization provides assistance to family caregivers of adults suffering from memory loss.

Family Caregivers Association
9621 E. Bexhill Dr.
Kensington, MD 20895-3104
(800) 535-3198
www.nfcacares.org
This is a national not-for-profit membership organization. Dues are $20 a year. It offers a support network, a speaker's bureau, and a quarterly newsletter.

Kate's Place2 Web Site
home.earthlink.net/~katesdrm/
Created by people who have been through the caregiving experience, this site's pages are sincere and personal. The site has an Internet relay chat room for caregivers.

Well Spouse Foundation
P.O. Box 801
New York, NY 10023
(212) 644-1241
This nonprofit group provides a bimonthly newsletter and referrals, information, and support to people caring for an ill spouse.

A WORD ABOUT GOVERNMENT-FUNDED PROGRAMS

A great deal of assistance is available from government agencies and groups that operate with some government funding.

As you're probably already well aware, dealing with government offices can be time consuming and frustrating. But keep dialing those telephone numbers or stopping at those agencies. It will be worth your trouble if you really need help. Others are getting the assistance those programs provide.

You may find that you or your relative qualify for some services, but not others. Some programs, even if you meet their criteria, have long waiting lists for services. Stick with that wait. Those lists change frequently, and names rise to the top as elders move, die, or find services elsewhere.

CAUTION

Don't take no for an answer if you know for a fact that a particular government program exists. You may be talking to an uninformed or misinformed staff person. Ask someone else—perhaps a supervisor—and keep asking until your request has been granted or your question answered to your satisfaction. No one in that office cares about your getting whatever that agency is offering more than you.

Help from government offices is often free. You may also find what is called a sliding-scale fee for that product or service, which is a charge based on a person's ability to pay.

If you don't qualify for any government-funded programs and you really need the service, you or your loved one will simply have to find the money in your own pockets. That's where this book comes in. We'll tell you how much things cost and where the money might come from to pay for them, and we'll help you assess your own financial situation, as well as that of your loved one.

Where financial planning is concerned, leave no stone unturned! Every little bit of assistance received will help.

PRINTED MATERIAL AND ON-LINE RESOURCES

These days a growing number of caregiver books, like this one, provide specific information, hints, and resources, whereas others are first-person accounts of a caregiver's experiences with someone dear to him or her. You may find comfort in these stories.

Other printed material includes magazines, newspapers and newsletters, pamphlets, and fact sheets published by associations, universities, research groups, and government agencies.

If you have a computer and modem, all you need is a service provider to tap into the Internet. As you may recall from the beginning of this chapter, the Internet now has thousands of resources for caregivers.

▼ **DID YOU KNOW . . .**
If you don't have access to a computer or are unfamiliar with the Internet, visit your public library. Most libraries have computers connected to the Internet that you can use, and a librarian will help you.

Some Web sites on the Internet have caregiver chat rooms that are busy into the wee hours of the morning—often the only time caregivers have time to themselves. Participants discuss specific problems they face and seek answers from those who have already faced such problems and may have solutions. Or they simply vent their emotions to people who understand exactly what they are going through. Some caregivers dislike chat rooms, dismissing them as a place for "whiners." Search around until you find one you are comfortable with.

▼ **CAUTION**
While the World Wide Web is a potpourri of information and support, it's just like the real world—filled with shysters and misinformation. Tread lightly—be careful.

RESOURCES IN THE LEAST LIKELY PLACES

One-on-one support also can come from coworkers, friends, support groups, hospital or nursing home staff, and disease-specific organizations (such as the American Heart Association).

Caring for a parent is something not many people discuss with coworkers, but there's no reason for that, considering the number of working caregivers. Many of your friends will *not* understand what you are going through, but many will; embrace them. A growing number of companies now sponsor support groups for employees. Check with the human resource manager to see if your company has one.

In the professional arena, you'll find many dedicated, loving, and caring social workers, discharge planners, and nurses. This is a group of people who *really* know the ropes. If you're lucky, you'll find one and, in him or her, a compassionate, empathetic friend who can take your hand and guide you through much of the caregiving maze.

SUPPORT GROUPS

Support groups can be a lifesaver. Here are people who are in your shoes, some who have worn the soles down considerably. In a support group you will find a place to express your feelings, realize that your problems are not unique, discover solutions, and, best of all, encounter a new circle of friends. Support group participants often trade caregiving duties with one another, allowing each other a respite. Some have speakers at each meeting from whom you may learn how to cope or get information about a new product or service that can help you. Here you will also learn about new federal, state, and local programs that can help. If you don't like a particular support group, find another one. A support group is as good as the people in it.

If you can't find one in your community, call or write the American Self-Help Clearinghouse, St. Clare's Riverside Medical Center, 25 Pocono Road, Denville, NJ 07834, (973) 625-7101.

INTRODUCTION TO SOME TERMS

The following are terms you will read often throughout this book and hear during your caregiving experience. This is not a comprehensive list, and new terms introduced in subsequent chapters will be explained there.

caregiver: This is a person who provides direct care of a loved one on a part-time or full-time basis. This term is used primarily to describe a layperson, but sometimes it is applied to a professional, such as a nurse or a social worker.

care manager: This is a person who oversees the care of a loved one on an occasional, part-time, or full-time basis. This term often implies a professional, but more and more is being used for laypersons as well.

case manager: This is a professional who manages a patient's progress in an institution from admittance to discharge. Formerly called a *discharge planner* and sometimes called a *care manager,* this person usually is either a social worker or a nurse. All major hospitals have them, as do many nursing homes and assisted-living facilities. Associations and nonprofit agencies employ them, too. Case managers represent the patient and most have dozens of patients at one time. They may be members of the National Association of Case Managers, which has requirements for membership. A resource is Aging Network Resources, 4400 E. West Highway, Suite 907, Bethesda, MD 20814. This company provides referrals to local care managers, but charges a fee for its services.

elder law attorney: This type of attorney specializes in the complex needs of seniors, and is, therefore, usually well versed in the ins and outs of Medicaid and Medicare, estate law, and wills and probate. The National Academy of Elder Law Attorneys was formed in 1988 by the American Bar Association to provide certification for this special group of lawyers. To become certified, attorneys must pass a grueling daylong test in elder law. If an attorney claims to be an elder law attorney, ask to see his or her certification. The association can be reached at (520) 881-4005 or www.nale.org. It can verify members or provide the names of elder law attorneys in your area.

geriatric care manager: This person performs the duties of a caregiver or a care manager for a fee. Though usually hired by the family caregiver, the geriatric care manager works for the elderly person who is being cared for. The field is unregulated in most states, so no license or special education is required. Many geriatric care managers are social workers, attorneys, psychologists, or registered nurses. At the minimum, the person should have a business license and liability insurance. Before hiring one, ask for personal and professional references and check them out thoroughly. Geriatric care managers charge by the hour or by the job. Their fees range from $40 to $100 an hour. The National Association of Professional Geriatric Care Managers has standards of practice that its members must meet. It maintains a list of members by state and will send you the names of members in your area. Call the group at (520) 881-8008.

CHAPTER TWO

$

Should You Be the *Caregiver* or the *Caretaker*?

I n Chapter 1 you read a lot about caregivers. Here, we introduce a new word: *caretaker.* A caretaker oversees care, rather
than providing it directly. Determining which role to take
requires serious thought and soul-searching. Finances, time,
proximity, mental health, and physical stamina all come into
play. This need not be an all-or-nothing situation. You can be a
part-time or occasional caregiver or caretaker, too.

▼▼▼

This we know: All things are connected,
like the blood which unites one family . . .
Chief Seattle, of the Dwamish Tribe (1786?–1866)

▲▲▲

If you have time to make this decision while your parents or
loved ones are still healthy, all the better. But sometimes caregivers
are suddenly thrust into their role. For instance, if your mother
has a severe, debilitating stroke, there may not be time to think
about whether you should be her caregiver. You simply react and
take care of her, or arrange for that care. However, when things
quiet down, be sure to give this question your full attention. Ideally, families should discuss this well in advance of need.

One woman, the president of a home health care company, saw firsthand the ravages of caregiving. Although she and her mother had a good relationship, she couldn't picture herself in a caregiving role. She discussed those feelings with Mom. Her mother agreed: She would not feel comfortable having her head-strong daughter making her decisions. Together they planned how care would be arranged for Mom, should the need ever arise. Mom saw an elder law attorney. She set up a trust, signed advance directives (legal documents that make your health care wishes known), made a will, and tried to provide for every contingency. (These topics are discussed in Chapters 10 and 18.) Mom wanted her daughter to be a limited caretaker, and this arrangement relieved them both.

In the preceding example, both parent and adult child were open to a frank discussion and preplanning.

AM I READY TO BE A CAREGIVER?

The truth is, not everyone can or should be a caregiver, the person who takes responsibility for the care. There are many reasons why you may not want this responsibility: You live far away from the loved one, you have a job and a family of your own, you have been estranged from the loved one, the person is difficult to manage—physically or mentally, your own life is unstable, or you just don't feel comfortable taking charge of another person's life, even if it is a family member.

If you conclude that you cannot be the caregiver, don't feel guilty or sad. It's better to recognize this about yourself now than later when the situation may worsen. It may even be helpful to have a frank talk with family members to discuss this, especially if you are the "chosen child," the sibling to whom duty always falls. (This chapter includes a discussion on family dynamics.)

However, don't think that because you have decided not to be the primary caregiver you can't still participate. Many families share caregiving duties, especially when an elderly parent is the care recipient. This distributes the workload among many instead of fixing it on one person. Plans such as this usually work best when siblings get along.

Here's an example of how one family shared caregiving duties. All four children elected to be caregivers for their elderly widowed father, who had suffered a stroke. One child, an accountant who lived in a neighboring state, took over finances. A daughter living nearby visited daily on her way home from work. She also enlisted Dad's friends and neighbors to check in on him each morning. Another daughter, already caring for an elderly mother-in-law, asked her teenage children to do housecleaning and yard work on weekends, paying them out of her own pocket. Another son lived across the country; he helped pay for extra expenses.

Every few months or so, the family held a telephone conference to discuss their father's needs and condition. The daughter who lived nearby always included Dad in the discussions, being careful to find out what he wanted and needed. Working together, they had a viable solution.

OR SHOULD I BE THE CARETAKER?

As you know, not all families work that well together, and in many instances there is only one child. When this is the case and that only child is you, you might want to consider being the caretaker by overseeing or directing care. A caretaker might arrange for home health care or custodial care, or research and arrange housing options. She or he might interview and hire a geriatric care manager who becomes the hands-on caregiver, but reports back to the caretaker.

A caretaker often lives a good distance from the loved one. Chapter 3, on long-distance caregiving, offers strategies if you fit into this category.

Becoming the caretaker doesn't mean you can't provide some care. You could hire a geriatric care manager, but still visit your loved one daily or weekly at a nursing home, bringing goodies or just spending quality time.

Furthermore, not all caregiving situations are as cut-and-dried as delineating between caregiver and caretaker. Sometimes you can be both.

▼ CAUTION
Never promise a family member that you will never place him or her in a nursing home. Good intentions and devotion can cause emotional trauma later if you are unable to keep that promise. A person with serious medical problems or Alzheimer's disease, someone who is combative or abusive, or someone who is too heavy to handle at home may have to be placed in a nursing home for his or her own good. Also, caregivers may develop medical problems themselves and be unable to provide hands-on care.

Here's how caregiving and caretaking worked for one career woman. After Mom fell and broke her hip, the daughter flew back and forth between two eastern seaboard states to help her. But the daughter could not continue to properly care for her mother while she was 1,000 miles away. After the daughter moved Mom into her own home and arranged daily care while she worked, her mother began acting peculiar. She was diagnosed with dementia. Mom's condition worsened, and the daughter, who was single, was unable to keep her at home and still work. A geriatric care manager explored their options. The care manager recommended that Mom be moved to a nursing home specializing in memory loss and helped the daughter select a sterling one nearby.

The care manager continues to oversee Mom's care, but the daughter has lunch with her mother nearly every weekday, takes her for strolls in a wheelchair on weekends, and occasionally takes her home.

SHARING THE JOB

As you have seen, neither role has to be a full-time job. While caretakers may spend less time at the task since they oversee care, there are ways to cut back on their tasks, too. Perhaps a claims service could file and check health insurance claims. You'll read more about that in Chapter 15.

As for the caregiver, you've read about how the care of a loved one can be spread among siblings, other relatives, and friends.

FAMILY DYNAMICS

As you begin thinking about caregiving, you need to include those closest to you—your family. Some caregivers say the hardest part of caregiving is dealing with one or more extended families. An adult child—maybe even you—may want to take over Mom and Dad's affairs to assist them; a spouse may want to continue to care for the loved one at home.

When siblings are involved, the decision-making process can become even more difficult. Siblings can disagree on a course of action for their parents and, when an extended family is present, multiple perspectives abound.

▼▼▼

Family quarrels are bitter things. They don't go by any rules.
They're not like aches or wounds; they're more like splits in the
skin that won't heal because there's not enough material.
F. Scott Fitzgerald, THE CRACK UP *(1945)*

▲▲▲

There's no one right way to deal with these matters. After all, every family is unique.

The best advice is to head off problems before they begin, by communicating effectively. If your parents or spouse are well, now is the time to ask about their future. Ask what are their wishes, should they need help or care. Unfortunately, many elders do not want to discuss this. People of their era did not discuss money or death, even with family members.

▼ **DID YOU KNOW . . .**
  Families fear discussions about money and the future because they raise difficult emotional issues such as aging and mortality, according to a 1997 study by Prudential Securities, entitled "Families and Money."

Quite truthfully, wills and advance directives (you'll read more about these in Chapters 10 and 18) are far from our minds when we are well and see no immediate need for them. This is true for all of us, so why should your parents feel differently? But you could ask them specific questions that aren't addressed in those legal documents. For example, "Would you want to live in Florida with Mary if you couldn't remain alone in your home?" "What do you think about assisted living?" "Does a retirement center or a smaller home appeal to you?"

SEEKING SOLUTIONS

One way to handle a potentially volatile family disagreement over someone's care is a family powwow. Let's pick a common situation and then seek a solution using this method.

Mom, a widow, lives in the two-story, four-bedroom home that she has lived in for 40 years, the house where she raised her children. She needs help with housekeeping and yard work. Though in fairly good health, vision problems prevent her from driving. Her three biological children are concerned about her living alone. A stepchild contends she is fine and should be allowed to live her life as she pleases. When the children come home for Thanksgiving, they notice Mom hasn't been eating and is losing weight.

What to do? First choose a leader, a person who will act as facilitator. He or she should keep family discussions focused and become the family "diplomat."

The family diplomat talks to Mom and learns that she is concerned about her inability to function independently. She doesn't eat much, she says, because it's no fun to cook for one person, and preparing meals is too much trouble. Still, she doesn't want to leave her home and the neighborhood where she knows everybody. Though she can't drive, stores are a few blocks away, and she has a friend who gives her a ride now and then to the doctor's office.

She is comfortable with a family discussion, as long as her desires are considered. She wants her family to be happy. She doesn't want them to fight or worry about her.

The diplomat notifies all the siblings, as well as a close aunt and uncle who live nearby. They agree to meet at Mom's. At the meeting, the diplomat states the problems objectively, cites Mom's wishes, and asks how they can accommodate her wishes.

As problems are stated, solutions form and the siblings learn more about Mom's finances. She volunteers that she can afford a housecleaning service and someone to take care of the yard, but she worries that spending money now will put her financially at risk if she lives 20 more years. This leads to a discussion on living past age 85, and Mom volunteers that she doesn't want to be kept alive by artificial means. That revelation allows a child to ask if Mom has advance directives. She admits she does not.

By the time the gathering is over, the family has solutions to the problems they face and an understanding of Mom's finances and wishes—for now and the future. Mom has agreed to pay for weekly cleaning. The children enlist a neighbor's teenage son to tend the yard. Mom's friend agrees to be the taxi service whenever Mom needs her. They arrange with a pharmacy and the neighborhood grocer to deliver prescriptions and groceries. The aunt and uncle agree to take Mom to dinner at least twice a month. The children will visit and call more frequently. Mom's support system is formed without a family quarrel—and with her wishes intact.

In that scenario, everything worked out well. Unfortunately, this is not always the case. Some families simply cannot agree or are carrying too much emotional baggage around with them. That's where a geriatric care manager can help. This person can objectively assess the situation, consult with the loved one, and then make recommendations with the loved one's best interest in mind.

If the loved one is not competent and the children still disagree on a plan for his or her care, a child may ask that a legal guardian be appointed. A legal guardian is someone (a relative or unrelated person) appointed by a court to oversee all or part of a person's life. (Chapter 18 explains legal guardianship.) A court proceeding can be a long, drawn-out affair if there is disagreement among immediate family members. Families should avoid this path unless they simply cannot reach consensus.

Some siblings agree to let one child take over the care and to abide by that person's decisions. This works well when the chosen child lives near the parent and has a flexible work schedule and family life, and the other siblings live in other states. This arrangement also works when siblings trust one another.

Even when a parent has prearranged for one child to care for him or her, jealousy can rear its ugly head. One family, consisting of two brothers and their mother, had some tense times over the mother's care. The mother named the eldest son executor of her estate. When the mother developed Alzheimer's disease, the eldest son took over her finances. But this son lived a good distance from Mom, whereas the younger son lived next door. Close proximity gave the younger son a better understanding of his mother's needs. The brothers often disagreed on her care, which created resentment between them, much of it stemming from childhood sibling rivalry. Fortunately, the mother remains well cared for, both financially and physically. The brothers, now in their mid-50s, are growing further apart.

KEEP COMMUNICATION LINES OPEN

Frank and open communications help where family dynamics are concerned. Siblings should put aside their differences and keep the parent's best interest in mind at all times.

▼▼▼

Birds in their little nests agree,
And 'tis a shameful sight
When children of one family
Fall out, and chide, and fight.
Isaac Watts, SONG XVII
(1674–1748)

▲▲▲

When siblings disagree, an independent third party—elder law attorney, trusted friend, geriatric care manager, or minister, priest, or rabbi—should be called in.

So which will you be—the caregiver or the caretaker? If you are still unsure, Figure 2.1 lists some points to consider during the decision-making process. Many of these are easily decided; emotional issues may take more soul-searching.

FIGURE 2.1 COULD I BE A CAREGIVER?

STATEMENT	NO	YES
1. I get along well with my loved one who needs care.		
2. We have an open relationship and can talk frankly about delicate matters, including health and finances.		
3. I could live with my loved one under the best conditions.		
4. I could live with my loved one under the worst conditions.		
5. My loved one has habits, such as smoking, that irritate me.		
6. My family (spouse/children) gets along well with my loved one.		
7. My family will support me in my decision.		
8. I have the time to devote to another dependent family member.		
9. My own health is good.		
10. I won't resent sacrificing my free time for my loved one.		
11. I can provide, or I am willing to learn, limited medical care, such as changing bandages or treating bedsores.		
12. I would feel comfortable bathing, dressing, diapering, or feeding my loved one.		
13. My finances would allow me to contribute when necessary.		
14. My employer would understand if I was late for work or if I left early or suddenly during the day because of caregiving duties and emergencies.		

If you answered no to half or more of these statements, you should consider being a caretaker rather than a caregiver.

I'VE DECIDED—NOW WHAT?

If you decide to be the caregiver, you have many things to consider and much to learn. Will the loved one live in your home or will you live in the loved one's home? Can your home or the loved one's home be renovated to accommodate two households, ensuring that each has breathing room? If you work, who will look after your loved one while you're gone, assuming he or she needs constant care? What services will be helpful to both of you to ensure safety and peace of mind? How will you and your loved one pay for these services?

The list is long and is different for each caregiver's and care receiver's situation. You'll find answers to many of these questions in the upcoming chapters.

As you have learned in this chapter, there are no hard and fast rules when it comes to caregiving. Do what works best for you and your loved one. And remember that conditions can and will change, often suddenly. You may be able to care for a loved one today, but not tomorrow. Changes in your and your loved one's health, finances, stability, and support may occur, changing your role from caregiver to caretaker, or even vice versa. With this in mind, a working plan should include the future—and all of its possibilities.

CHAPTER THREE

Moving? Long-Distance Caregiving? What's Best Right Now

Deciding how to care for a loved one when you live some distance away is difficult. Your first instinct may be to relocate immediately to where the person is—if not into his or her house, then at least to that town.

Or your initial reaction could be to ask the person to move where you are.

Or you might try to care for the person long distance.

Which is the right approach?

Three caregivers might make three different choices. There is no one *right* way, only the system that works for you and your loved one *right now*. That could change. For example, you might be a long-distance caregiver for a time while the person remains at home, and when that is no longer effective, the individual could move to your home or community.

Many factors enter into your decision on this important, and potentially expensive, subject. This chapter will help you with the quandary of the three choices mentioned earlier.

WHAT DOES YOUR LOVED ONE THINK?

Before getting into housing decisions, here's an important point to consider.

The suggestions offered throughout this book may seem to be directed to you as if you were making them alone, with no input from your care recipient. Perhaps that's the case. However, if the care recipient is able to express a preference—in housing, in elder services, in any aspect of his or her life—then naturally the person's opinions should be taken into account. Perhaps they are not viable suggestions, and you might need to have your relative talk with a lawyer, a counselor for seniors, or some other professional in order to see the wisdom of pursuing a course other than the one he or she prefers. But generally speaking, keep in mind that your relative, like everyone else, wants some control over his or her life and should be accorded that right if at all possible.

The loved one you're caring for might be 85 years old, in relatively good health, and sharp as a tack. Or the person could be 62 and in the advanced stages of Alzheimer's disease. That's certainly a wide range of cognitive ability. You should adapt the advice in these pages to your own particular care recipient's abilities.

▼▼▼

One often contradicts an opinion when it is really only the tone in which it has been presented that is unsympathetic.
Friedrich Nietzsche, Human, All Too Human *(1878)*

▲▲▲

MOVING TO BE NEAR YOUR CARE RECIPIENT

Here are some considerations if you think you might want to relocate to be closer to whomever you're caring for.

FAMILY

If you are married or in a serious relationship, how willing is your partner to move? Do you have children? Are they at an age where it will be relatively easy to uproot them, or can you leave them behind if they are adults?

JOB

This is an important factor for both you and your partner, especially if you are taking on some or all of the care recipient's living expenses, as well as continuing to pay your own.

- Does your company have an office in or near the loved one's town? Could you manage a transfer there?
- If that's not feasible, what about jobs in the new locale? Are job prospects good in your field?
- Will you have to take a cut in pay? If so, can you meet all of your expenses living there?
- Can you afford the moving costs?

HOUSING

If you are now renting, you might have to break a lease in order to move. This could be an expensive proposition if the landlord demands that you pay the rent for the months remaining in the term of the lease. If your landlord does not want to let you out of the lease—and moving to be near an ailing parent is not a frivolous reason for requesting your release—ask if he or she will do so if you find a tenant for that apartment, someone who will either sublet it or sign a new lease. The landlord may agree to this solution. Don't just pick up and leave. The landlord could sue you for breaking a legal contract. If the landlord does sue, you might have to pay the total rent for the balance of the lease, plus legal costs.

If you plan to rent when you move, remember to factor higher rent into your budgeting. In addition, you may need two months' security deposit and a pet deposit of $100 or more if you plan to bring Fido or Mittens along. If you're renting a $600-a-month apartment or house, the up-front money needed could be as much as $2,500, when you include the first month's rent, too. There are the usual setting-up expenses attached to moving, such as utilities, telephone, and cable television hookup. Don't forget the move itself, which can cost several hundred, or a few thousand, dollars.

If you want to buy a house or condominium in or near your relative's community, look into housing prices there while you're still in your present home. Will they be less than what you are paying now? Or—bad news—is it just the reverse? For instance, moving from a house or a condo in a small town in the Midwest to a pricey city like San Francisco or New York is going to be expensive, whether you're buying or renting. You may wind up living farther from your relative than you would like, just to find an affordable neighborhood or town. Or you might have to move in with the person even if that's not your preference.

If you plan to sell a house or condominium, will you make a profit or at least break even on the transaction? If housing prices are flat or depressed where you are moving from, you might have to take a loss on the sale. Unless a move is imperative immediately, you may want to wait until the local real estate market picks up.

Finally, if you move in with someone, will you be taking over the mortgage or rent payments? What about other housing expenses, such as real estate taxes, condo fees, and utilities?

Leaving your home and its expenses and moving into someone else's home and paying for housing could be a draw money-wise, or the bottom line could show a gain or a loss for you. Figure 3.1 is a worksheet to help you determine the expenses you are likely to incur if you move (as far as you can project at this planning stage).

EMOTIONS

Of course, emotional issues are nowhere near as clear-cut an element of your move as working with numbers. As you have read in the preceding chapters, a family dynamic exists for every caregiver. For example, if you choose to move to your relative's home, is that what the relative wants? Indeed, are *you* going willingly, or with resentment? By all means, talk things over with the person to avoid the sort of misunderstanding that results in a move that doesn't work for either of you.

FIGURE 3.1 THE DOLLARS AND CENTS OF MOVING

Try to estimate as closely as possible the expenses in the two choices involved in moving to be closer to your loved one. Include in your calculations any costs you expect your care recipient to carry or pay in part. There's no right answer here—the most expensive decision may still be the better choice for you right now. It's just important to see the financial implications of your decision on paper.

	YOUR MONTHLY EXPENSES NOW	IF YOU'LL LIVE *WITH* THE CARE RECIPIENT AND PAY SOME OR ALL EXPENSES (ESTIMATE WHAT YOU'LL PAY)	IF YOU'LL LIVE *NEAR* THE CARE RECIPIENT AND HELP WITH EXPENSES (ESTIMATE EXPENSES FOR BOTH OF YOU)
Rent			
Security deposit			
Pet fee			
Mortgage payment			
Down payment, closing costs on new place*			
Related housing expenses (real estate taxes, insurance, condo fees, heat, A/C, etc.)			
Other			
Food			
Medical			
Entertainment			
Transportation			
Other			
TOTAL			

Your monthly income _____

Care recipient's monthly income** _____

TOTAL INCOME _____

(Check total income against expenses you will have in columns 2 and 3)

Moving costs* _____ _____

* If you are a homeowner, these expenses, and others connected with your move, could be offset by any profit you realize from the sale of your present home.
** If you know this figure or the care recipient is willing to give you the information. Don't push for it.

If you will be moving back to your hometown, do you have siblings in that area? Are they supportive, or do you anticipate ongoing hassles? If you're walking into the latter situation, can you cope with those feelings along with your new job of caring for your loved one and his or her increasing needs?

HAVING YOUR RELATIVE MOVE IN WITH YOU

Having your relative live with you might be the more workable scenario for you. The following sections discuss the same considerations as in the previous scenario, but this time as they apply to having your relative move to your town, perhaps even into your home.

FAMILY

Is everyone in agreement about having the care recipient as a live-in member of the family? If you are hearing (or sensing) serious reservations from your partner, or if your home is just too small for another person, you might consider having your loved one rent an apartment in your community. There's more about that later in this chapter.

If everyone agrees to let the loved one move into your home (or neither you nor your parent can afford an apartment for him or her elsewhere in town), you can adapt your home easily, with little change to the existing dwelling, or you can pull out the stops. For instance, you might build the first-floor addition you have always wanted. You can learn more about both choices in the next few pages, under "Adapting Your Home to the Newcomer's Needs."

JOB

Employment shouldn't be an issue if your parent moves in order to be near you. Presumably, your parent is not working or will soon retire. If work, whether part-time or temporary, *is* an important consideration, you might want to scout the employment field before your parent arrives.

▼ CAUTION

Be realistic. Avoid painting too rosy a picture of part-time work, only to have your loved one's hopes dashed when he or she sees the *real* employment picture in your community. That major disappointment could seriously affect the person's ability to settle in.

Work probably won't change much for you now that your loved one is living with you or in your town. In fact, you may lose less time now that you don't have to leave town when problems develop with the person where he or she is now. Chapter 4 discusses the federal Family and Medical Leave Act and how you can adapt its provisions as needed when you're on the job. Chapter 13 will help you get a support team in place when your loved one arrives, so that you can work with a reasonably free mind. Chapter 13 is directed at helping your loved one stay in his or her home, but its suggestions are applicable to you if your relative moves in with you or even into your town.

HOUSING AND EMOTIONS

Before asking a loved one to live with you, be certain that everyone in the household can get along reasonably well (admittedly, this is hard to tell before setting up your multigenerational household). It's especially important that *you* get along with your loved one, since you are the caregiver.

There are clues as to how successful this arrangement is likely to be. Chapter 2 mentioned family dynamics and, siblings notwithstanding, you are pretty clear about the relationship that exists between you and your loved one. For example, perhaps there was always friction between the two of you, and you carry unresolved conflicts from years past. Or maybe you have noticed in the last few years, now that you are both older, that some of the jagged edges have been smoothed, and you've reached a new understanding—or, at least, acceptance. Or perhaps you find that, because of the loved one's failing health, your worried and sometimes harried visits, money concerns and other problems (whether yours or your relative's), tensions between the two of you have exacerbated.

If you just *know* that this move will not work out, consider asking your relative to move to your town, where, if it's an affordable option, all parties involved will shop for an attractive apartment for the person. If that is not feasible, consider counseling for yourself or the loved one, or seek the aid of a caregivers' support group, which can help you work out a viable under-one-roof living situation.

Here's a suggestion: Your relative may want to move to a senior citizens rental building in your community. There is a full discussion of this housing style in Chapter 13.

There is still another possibility. Your loved one might consider a move to a continuing care retirement community (known as a CCRC) in or near your town. An assisted-living facility is another answer. Chapter 14 has a full explanation of these housing styles. They can work for fairly healthy seniors, as well as for those who need some assistance with daily living or even full-time nursing care.

ADAPTING YOUR HOME
TO THE NEWCOMER'S NEEDS

In a house or a condominium, the changeover can be as simple as having your relative take a spare bedroom or the room of one of your kids who is now independent. If yours is a two-story home and your relative can't manage stairs, you might purchase a chairlift that runs along the stairway or, if you have a den or other extra room on the ground floor, that could become the person's living quarters.

> ▼ **DID YOU KNOW . . .**
> To make your home adaptable for a handicapped family member—by, for example, adding a wheelchair ramp or

widening doorways—check the yellow pages under "Handicapped Accessibility" for contractors with that specialty. If you can't afford such adaptations, call the national Eldercare Locator at (800) 677-1116 for the names of groups or agencies in your area that help at no charge. Many of these changes are tax deductible.

Someone with a private home could convert a two-car garage to a *bedsitter*—a living room with a convertible sofa or Murphy bed (a bed that is stored vertically along a wall and pulls down from that position when needed). The area also usually contains a bath. A one-car garage might be transformed into a bedroom. Perhaps you have an empty room over the garage, which is a possible solution if the care recipient can navigate the stairs and if there's room to install a bath.

A local contractor can give you quotes for the cost of such renovations. Depending on the size of the space and how plain or lavish you want to make those living areas, you can expect to pay anywhere from around $2,000 to convert a one-car garage to a bedroom to perhaps $8,000 or more for a room and bath in your garage or extensive renovation to existing space in the top half of that structure.

Another option is building a bedroom and bath addition to your ground floor. Check with your local zoning office to see if that is allowed in your particular neighborhood and to find out how you should proceed (permits, inspection of the new construction by the city, etc.). How much you spend for an addition depends, again, on how simple or posh you want that wing to be. A minimum cost for a mother-in-law room with bath might be $15,000 to $20,000, depending on floor plans and materials used. Some housing additions can end up costing well over $100,000.

▼! CAUTION
Be careful that an addition won't make your home the largest on the block. That could affect your ability to sell it when you want to and at a price satisfactory to you. The

most expensive house in a neighborhood is usually not as good an investment as one that fits in with the rest of the homes, price- and sizewise.

There is yet another alternative when considering renovation. If your loved one is still more or less able to live independently (with some occasional help from you) and prefers to do so—and if it sounds like a good solution to have your relative close by but with some distance between you—you may be able to convert part of your house to a full apartment. A full apartment contains a kitchen, however small—that is, not just a room or two and a bath. You will certainly have to seek zoning board approval for such a conversion, which may or may not be granted for a home on your particular block or in your immediate neighborhood. If it's not, you can apply for a variance to allow you to proceed with the remodeling, although that, too, might be denied.

Don't stop there. In some towns you can make the conversion if you do not change the exterior of your home—that is, if you don't create a second exterior entrance. You might also be permitted to create an apartment if it's needed for a close relative. In such a case, the town might require that when the relative moves out or dies, the house revert to its original single-family status. Call your local zoning office to inquire about those options.

Will building a wing on your house or creating a full apartment there, which would make your residence into a two-family home, increase your real estate taxes?

You'll be in a for a new assessment of your home. If you have built a wing that makes the house larger than it was initially, you are likely to be handed a higher property tax bill. Some communities reassess the value of residential properties only at 7- or 10-year intervals, so you might have a long wait for word of an increased tax. In other parts of the country, a property is reassessed every time it is sold. Occasionally, the fact that a homeowner is seeking a building permit will "red flag" that property for reassessment. It's best to call your local tax assessor's office to find out just what the policy is in your town and when the next communitywide reassessment is scheduled.

WHERE THE RENOVATION MONEY MIGHT COME FROM

Whether you furnish a room in your home for your care recipient or build a new wing for the person, there are likely to be expenses attached to the move. Perhaps these expenses will be minor and you'll be able to absorb them fairly easily. Maybe the relative could pay all or some of them, or help with payments on an improvement loan. If you're working the numbers and can't see where to come up with the money you need, turn to Chapter 8, which explains various sources for obtaining cash when you need it.

There's one source for borrowing that should be mentioned here: Title 1 loans, available from the federal government under the auspices of the Federal Housing Administration (FHA). These loans carry lower-than-market interest rates, and you don't have to have an FHA-backed mortgage to secure one—you can hold a conventional home loan. Call your regional office of the U.S. Department of Housing and Urban Development for more information. HUD is in your telephone book in the federal government listings.

A final resource is *Where to Get Grants and Loans to Repair and Remodel Your Home*, a 192-page paperback published by the Consumer Education Research Center (1997). The book lists over 7,000 sources of loans and grants offered by all levels of government, by utility companies, and by others. It provides explanations of these programs, eligibility requirements, form letters for applying, and instructions for determining your debt-to-income ratio for eligibility. The book costs $19.95 plus $3 for shipping and is available from the Consumer Education Research Center at 1980 Springfield Ave., Maplewood, NJ 07040, (973) 275-3955 or (800) USA-0121, or on-line at www.planet.net\cerc.

LONG-DISTANCE CAREGIVING

Your third caregiving option is looking after your loved one from your home, while the person remains in his or her own home some miles away.

Long-distance caregiving might sound like the simplest solution—you stay in your home and the loved one stays in his or hers—but it brings its own set of concerns. Is the care recipient eating properly? Why didn't he or she answer the phone this morning? It's that kind of worry.

Nevertheless, this can work quite well. The key is having support services in place where the care recipient is. That can be in the form of a geriatric care manager (see Chapter 1) and/or a variety of local services, which are discussed in more detail in Chapter 13.

> ### ▼ DID YOU KNOW . . .
> If you take a phone book home with you from your care recipient's town, you can call your support team there, the local social services agencies, and the like, without spending money dialing information to get those numbers.

FILLING IN FOR YOU

You might want to select a secondary caregiver where your parent lives. This person's role will be to look in on your parent, call occasionally, check his or her home, be sure bills are being paid, supervise the services provided—make certain that your parent is getting meals-on-wheels (a low-cost meal plan that is explained in Chapter 13), that the volunteer from church is driving your parent to doctors' appointments, and so on. The secondary caregiver also reports regularly to you about your parent.

Whom can you select for that role? Ideally, someone your parent knows, perhaps a neighbor or a friend of either of you. It should go without saying that this will have to be a person both of you trust. He or she will have the keys to your parent's home and, if you choose, access to your parent's bank accounts for making deposits, paying bills, and so forth.

If you do find someone to take on that kind of financial responsibility, you will no doubt want to periodically check up on that person and monitor the record keeping.

How much you pay can depend on the services you are requesting. List what you want your other caregiver to do during the course of a week, and try to calculate how many hours that will take. How much will you pay the person an hour? Multiply that by the number of hours you expect the person to work in a week and you'll come up with a weekly wage. Or you could ask the secondary caregiver to keep track of hours, submitting a bill to you for payment weekly or biweekly.

DID YOU KNOW . . .
Several airlines now have a "compassionate fare" for discounted tickets if you must travel because of a serious illness in the family, which is in addition to the more commonly known "bereavement fare" for flying to a close relative's funeral.

Remember, if you pay your secondary caregiver more than $600 a year, you must file notice of that employment with the Social Security office, and you must pay unemployment insurance. Your accountant can help you with the paperwork.

Try to take a trip to your relative's hometown to set up your support network. It's certainly easier than doing it by phone. When you return home you may well have a higher phone bill each month as you keep in touch with your "staff" back there, but you'll know your parent is receiving the best care possible—and in his or her own home, too.

CHAPTER FOUR

$

Balancing Caregiving and Your Job

So you've decided to become a caregiver and continue to work. You will find yourself engaged in a constant juggling act, balancing caregiving duties and your job. The first step is to advise your employer that you are caring for a loved one. Explain that you may need to take more time off during work hours, but that you are willing to make up the time. Ask to use vacations, compensated time, and personal holidays to make up time you miss.

Typically this requires about six days a year to provide routine care, according to some estimates, and another three days to deal with eldercare crises. If you're an average working caregiver, you'll probably be arriving at work late, taking long lunch hours and leaving early, and making many phone calls on the job to the loved one and to service providers.

On the other hand, if your company offers eldercare benefits, the time you spend away from the job will be less. In 1997, 30% of the nation's employers offered eldercare benefits, up 13% from 1991, according to Hewitt Associates' annual 1996 survey.

Those companies provided benefits including information and referral services, 79%; long-term care insurance, 25%; counseling service, 17%; and other benefits, 9%. Some companies also offer in-house seminars on legal and financial matters for caregivers.

Employers offer these services because they face an estimated $11.4 billion in annual productivity losses from a growing number of employees caring for elderly relatives. Eldercare programs help employees cope, and you should take advantage of them; some may be extremely helpful as your caregiving progresses. If you're not sure whether your company offers eldercare services, ask the human resources manager.

COMPANY-PROVIDED INFORMATION AND REFERRAL SERVICES

Companies that provide eldercare benefits usually do so through an outside firm with expertise in the eldercare arena, although some of the largest companies have their own in-house eldercare providers. Services rendered by these eldercare firms are as good as the company or individual providing them.

Eldercare benefit companies may simply provide a list of applicable services in the town where you or your loved one lives, or they may investigate service providers and give you a shortlist of recommended companies from which to choose. Some take a full history of you and your loved one and make recommendations, whereas others may ask what you need and provide a list. Still others may hire a geriatric care manager who will work directly with you in assessing your situation and make appropriate recommendations. Often, the care manager will follow up to see how you are doing. The largest eldercare benefit firms even have eldercare attorneys, physicians, and social workers on their staffs.

BEFORE YOU "TAKE YOUR JOB AND SHOVE IT"

Some caregivers may find that, despite employer assistance, they are unable to continue working full-time. If you reach a point where quitting your job seems to be necessary, consider the impact this decision will have on your financial future. Unemployed, you likely will lose your health care benefits, put a dent in or lose your pension, lessen your Social Security earnings, and affect your overall retirement plan. You may be able to get by without your salary, but company-paid benefits and government benefits will also be affected. Before making a final decision, consider other options. You could ask your employer for a different position with less responsibility, flextime, or work that can be done from home.

▼▼▼

Change is the law of life. And those who look only to the past or the present are certain to miss the future.
John F. Kennedy, Address, Frankfurt, Germany,
June 25, 1963

▲▲▲

EXPLORING THE OPTIONS

A new position with less responsibility might give you the breathing room you need to cope with caregiver responsibilities. Maybe your hours will change, too, which could be a help.

Flextime will almost certainly allow time off in the mornings or afternoons to tend to family matters. Perhaps, if you can manage it, you might opt for a four-day, ten-hour workweek. The upside is an extra day home; the downside, additional stress during those long workdays. If a family member is available to help during weekends, perhaps you could work Tuesday through Saturday. If none of these options work for you or suit your employer, maybe you could work from home, as a growing number of workers do. Of course, your job must be one that can be done via computer and telephone. Your company may even pay for the equipment you will need. (If not, you'll probably have to spend $3,000 to $5,000 for a new computer, or about half that amount for a used computer.

For other alternatives contact New Ways to Work, 785 Market St., Suite 950, San Francisco, CA 94103, (415) 995-9860. This nonprofit group provides information on how caregivers can restructure their jobs.

MAYBE PART-TIME?

You might also consider working fewer hours as a part-time employee. Though many employers do not pay benefits to part-time workers, some may offer reduced benefits. For example, a part-time employee may still be eligible to participate in the company group health insurance plan, but the employee may have to pick up the employer's share of the premium. The same may apply to life insurance. And, unless you work from home, you will lose your disability insurance. Ask your human resources manager what is available to you.

On the plus side, working part-time may offset other expenses, such as a full day of adult day care or child care.

FAMILY AND MEDICAL LEAVE ACT

If salary is not as important as benefits, you may opt to invoke the Family and Medical Leave Act. This 1993 federal law requires companies that employ 50 or more workers within a 75-mile radius to allow workers up to 12 weeks off, without pay, in any 12-month period to care for seriously ill immediate family members. An immediate family member can be a parent, a spouse, or a child. (Employees who have serious health problems themselves may also use this plan.) Employees may take the entire 12 weeks at one time or spread it out over the year. If you take this leave, you are guaranteed the same position or one with equivalent pay, benefits, and other conditions of employment when you return.

Of course, there are exceptions. Employees in the highest-paid 10% of the workforce, where their absence would mean a substantial economic loss to the company, are eligible for a job when they return, but may be denied their former or a comparable job. So if you are a highly paid manager, there is no guarantee that you will have the same job at comparable pay when you return. Part-time employees' leave time is calculated on a proportional basis determined by the number of hours normally worked each week.

In addition, all employees who choose such leave must meet these conditions:

- The employee must have been employed with the company for at least 12 months and worked at least 1,250 hours during the preceding 12 months.

- The employee must have exhausted all vacation and all sick and personal leave accrued.

- The employee must contact his or her employer at least biweekly to advise the employer of his or her status and intent to return to work. If an employee advises the employer that he or she will not return to work, the employer is not required to continue its obligation.

- The employee must provide proof, if requested, that he or she or the person he or she is caring for is medically needy.

During your time off, you will still have to pay for your health care coverage or any other benefits to which you contributed a share while you were working. Your company must continue to pay its share, the same as if you were working. You may elect to drop those benefits to avoid paying the premiums; if you do so, your benefits will be restored when you return. But think twice before dropping benefits, especially health insurance.

FAMILY AND MEDICAL LEAVE ACT ADMINISTRATION

The Department of Labor, Employment Standards Administration, Wage and Hours Division, administrates the Family and Medical Leave Act. The Department of Labor, Employment Standards Division, oversees complaints and violations. Regional offices for both departments are listed in the white pages or in the government listing section of your local telephone book.

STATE FAMILY LEAVE ACTS

In addition to the federal law, many states now have family leave laws. Some may be more stringent than the federal law, but none can be less stringent. To find out if your state has such a law, contact the Department of Labor or a similar state agency.

CONSIDER A LEAVE OF ABSENCE

If you work for a company that is not required to honor the Family Leave and Medical Act because of its size, or if you need more than the 12 weeks offered under the act, you might consider asking your employer for a six-month or one-year leave of absence. Although no employer is required to offer such a leave, many do so on a routine basis for a good employee for good cause.

Such a leave will be without pay, and you will probably pick up all the costs of your benefits, if they are even made available to you. Find out how taking a leave of absence impacts your pension plan and your other benefits as well.

> **DID YOU KNOW . . .**
> Some states pay a small subsidy to people who stay home and care for a loved one. The subsidy costs the state less than having to pay for assisted living or nursing home care for a senior.

Talk to your immediate supervisor about such a possibility and make sure you understand the full costs involved. You should ask:

- How will this affect my health care and dental insurance costs and coverage?

- Will I be able to continue with my company's insurer? How much will I have to pay? If I cannot continue coverage, can I get coverage elsewhere? What will it cost? Will I be covered for preexisting conditions? When I return to work after the year is up, will I have to undergo a medical exam to reinstate coverage? Are benefits reduced?

- How will this affect my life insurance cost and coverage? Can the insurance be continued? How much will the premium be? Will I pay the full amount? Will I have to qualify again when I return? Can I take out a term life insurance policy while I'm on leave? What must I do to qualify? What will it cost?

- Will my disability insurance be terminated? What must I do to reinstate it when I return?

- How will this affect my company retirement and/or 401(k) plan?

Ask all of these questions before you take a leave of absence, go to part-time status, or quit your job. After all, benefits are important to your own future. If you have or develop health problems, you may find it difficult to get health care coverage after you drop your company plan.

Remember that under the federal Comprehensive Omnibus Budget Reconciliation Act, known as COBRA, you can remain in your group plan for 18 months or longer, if your previous employer has more than 20 employees; however, the premium will be 102% of your current cost. To qualify, you have to apply for benefits before your coverage ends.

Find out also what effect terminating employment or taking a leave of absence will have on your seniority and vacations. It would be devastating to have earned four weeks or more of vacation, and then return as a new employee with only one week of vacation time a year.

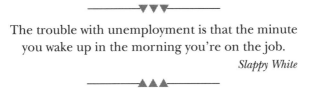

The trouble with unemployment is that the minute you wake up in the morning you're on the job.

Slappy White

EMPLOYEE ASSISTANCE PROGRAMS

Many large companies also have employee assistance programs to help employees through troubling times. While some programs are geared toward drug or alcohol addiction or child care, many provide counseling and legal services under this program umbrella.

Counseling may help you see your situation more clearly and may help you in assessing your caregiving situation. With this guidance, you might see options more clearly and make the decision that is best for you instead of the decision that is best for

FIGURE 4.1 CAN YOU AFFORD TO QUIT YOUR JOB?

My annual salary	$_____
My annual expenses	$_____
Difference (subtract expenses from salary)	$_____

How my salary could be replaced (use annual figures):

Savings (amount)	$_____
Stock earnings	$_____
Reduced costs	
Commuting costs (gas, toll, parking)	$_____
Dry cleaning	$_____
Clothing	$_____
Lunch	$_____
Transportation	$_____
Other wage earner	$_____
Total savings	$_____

Additional costs:

Health insurance	$_____
Life insurance	$_____
Dental insurance	$_____
Total additional	$_____

Intangible costs:
Loss of seniority
Loss of paid vacation
Social isolation
Affect on mental and physical health

Intangible rewards:
Caring for a loved one
Giving back to my parents
Drawing closer to a loved one

your loved one. A good counselor may also offer alternatives that help *both* you and your loved one.

A FEW WORDS ABOUT LONG-TERM SECURITY

Can you make it financially as an at-home caregiver? Only you can decide. You will want to determine how quitting your job might affect your financial future (see Figure 4.1). Financial planners stress three sources of funds for retirement: savings and investments, Social Security, and pensions. Of these three, your pension may be the most important. Unfortunately, if you quit your job, you could be jeopardizing your pension, as well as your Social Security—how much you receive when you retire is based on a number of factors, including how long you worked and how much you earned while working. And while it's true that you can put money away anytime, don't overlook the fact that savings grow faster by compounding earnings on money already in the bank. The longer you have to save, the more you'll have when you retire.

Before making a major decision, such as quitting your job, read Chapter 11, which has important information about your pension and savings.

CHAPTER FIVE

$

Taking Care of the Caregiver

The most common mistake caregivers make is not taking care of themselves. Support group facilitators, care managers, and social workers all report that caregivers forget about themselves. Could it be that caregivers forget that if they get sick or are unable to perform their duties, no one will be there to care for them?

The physical, mental, and even financial ramifications are clear. When the caregiver gets sick, the loved one will have to go to a nursing home or an assisted-living facility, and the cost is steep—$30,000 a year or more, not to mention the cost of doctor visits, medicine, and maybe even a hospital visit for the caregiver.

As is often the case in life, prevention is better than cure. Those who take on caregiving duties need to plan time for themselves, too. This means spending a few hours a day working in the garden, reading a novel, listening to music, watching television, or simply watching the wind blow leaves across the yard. It means getting out to visit friends, taking in a movie, having lunch or dinner out, going on a Saturday outing with family, spending at least a long weekend away from the loved one on a mini-vacation, or attending worship services.

And just how, you wonder, will you find time to do these things? The answer is simple: Make time and let others help. Build a network of friends, relatives, neighbors, and other caregivers to help you. Explore respite programs in your area. Take advantage of caregiver programs and seminars that provide free or low-cost care for loved ones. Let numerous organizations help you.

▼▼▼

Friendship . . . lightens adversity by
dividing it and sharing it.
Cicero, DE AMICITIA *(44 B.C.)*

▲▲▲

YOUR MENTAL HEALTH

After a time of intensive caregiving, it will be easy to begin feeling sorry for yourself. Your life is passing by, your friends are taking exotic vacations and you can't, the sailboat you bought hasn't been used in years, friends call less often because they know you can't go shopping or to a movie at the drop of a hat, and on and on goes your list of woes. Eventually, you could become depressed. Don't allow this to happen.

Tend to your mental health along the way. This won't be easy at first, but as you fall into the caregiving routine, look for ways to renew your spirit. One way is through humor.

LOOK AT THE FUNNY SIDE OF LIFE

Many caregivers are able to laugh at the antics of their loved ones. If Dad has Alzheimer's disease and he says something funny, laugh about it instead of being sad over his confusion and memory loss.

One caregiver gets a lot of mileage from a comment her mother made. Before Alzheimer's disease struck, mom had spent her retirement years going on cruises. After years of caring for her mother at home, the daughter had to place her in a nursing home. The home, with its wood rails in the halls and small, round windows, must have seemed like a cruise ship to Mom.

The first week the daughter came to visit, her mother told her, "This is a nice ship, but the service is the worst I've ever seen!"

KNOW THAT YOUR CAREGIVING IS AN ACT OF LOVE

If you have regarded your efforts as an act of love, then long after your loved one is gone, you can feel good about what you did. Many adult children are remorseful after their parents die that they didn't do enough for them when they were alive.

USE YOUR TIME TOGETHER TO GROW

Learn more about yourself, your loved one, and your family. One caregiver has tea each morning with her 90-something aunt who lives with her. During this time together, she has learned many things about her family and their past that she otherwise never would have learned.

BE CREATIVE

Look at caregiving as a challenge and see how creative you can be in rising to the call. If your loved one enjoys playing bridge and he is unable to go out, can you bring a bridge foursome home?

Stay in touch with friends and say "Yes!" when they ask, "Is there anything I can do to help?" Keep a list handy of things people can do to help you. Let someone play canasta with your parent while you go to a movie. Ask your neighbors to drop off your laundry when they drop off theirs. Tell friends that fresh cut flowers brighten your day, and ask them to bring roses from their garden.

JOIN A SUPPORT GROUP

This strategy cannot be stressed enough. Find a support group that meets regularly and is made up of people with whom you have something in common, whether it is caregiving, Alzheimer's disease, Parkinson's disease, or stroke recovery. Share your feelings, frustrations, and hard-won wisdom with them. Help start a respite program in your group, or agree to watch another caregiver's loved one while the caregiver gets out for a few hours, and then reciprocate.

TAKE A VACATION

Schedule yourself for a vacation. Make it a long weekend or a week. Check in your area for facilities that offer respite care, such as adult day care centers, retirement homes, church groups, and nursing homes.

START A CLUB

Start a book or card club and ask members to meet in your home. Explain to them that you have caregiving duties.

DEPRESSION

Sometimes, no matter what you do to protect your mental health, depression will creep in. Everyone becomes depressed now and then. Holidays, the death of a friend or loved one, rainy days, divorce, job loss, even long winters can trigger depression. Being depressed can mean feeling blue, sad, numb, or empty. For most of us, these feelings pass.

Should your depression linger, however, consider seeing a professional who can help you. A counselor, minister, psychologist, or psychiatrist can help. Some psychologists even specialize in treating caregivers and the elderly.

If you need help but don't know where to start, try some of these organizations:

> American Association for Marriage and Family Therapy
> 1100 17th St. NW, 10th Floor
> Washington, DC 20036
> (800) 374-2638
> This group provides referrals to professionals who can help caregivers and the elderly.

American Psychiatric Association
1400 K St. NW
Washington, DC 20005
(202) 682-6000
This organization provides free publications about mental
illness.

National Association of Social Workers
750 1st St. NE
Washington, DC 20002
(202) 408-8600
This group provides referrals to local therapists.

WARNING SIGNS OF CLINICAL DEPRESSION

✔ Persistent sadness or anxiety
✔ Feeling guilty, worthless, helpless, hopeless, or pessimistic
✔ Loss of interest or pleasure in hobbies, activities that you once
  enjoyed, or sex
✔ Insomnia, oversleeping, or waking early
✔ Weight loss or gain, loss of appetite or overeating
✔ Fatigue or energy loss
✔ Thoughts of death or suicide
✔ Feeling restless or irritable
✔ Difficulty concentrating, remembering, or making decisions
✔ Persistent physical symptoms that don't respond to treatment,
  such as headaches or chronic pain

YOUR PHYSICAL HEALTH

▼▼▼

Better to hunt in fields for health unbought
Than fee the doctor for a nauseous draught.

The wise for cure on exercise depend;
God never made his work for man to mend.
John Dryden (1631–1701),
Epistle to John Dryden of Chesterton
▲▲▲

With your sanity intact, you will be better able to care for yourself physically. Be sure to make and keep your own doctor appointments. Let your primary care physician know that you are a caregiver. Take vitamins to supplement missed or skimped meals and keep your energy level high.

Do you have an exercise program? Maybe jogging or tennis? If not, develop a five-minute routine, which can be as simple as stretches or as strenuous as a cardiovascular workout. Do it twice a day or more.

If you hate exercise (and many of us do), sneak it in by working in the yard. Mow the grass or pull weeds, plant a healing garden, or put in a fresh crop of vegetables. Let your loved one sit outside with you, if he or she is able, and enjoy the sunshine and breeze, too.

Ward off colds and flu when they start. Get a flu shot yourself when you take your care recipient to get one.

Get enough sleep. If you can't get it at night, work in power naps during the day or sleep when your loved one sleeps. The laundry will still be there when you wake up.

Caregivers also should consider a strength training program, especially if they will have to assist or lift a care recipient from a chair to bed or bath. Even changing sheets on a bedbound person's bed can exact a toll. Too many caregivers end up at the doctor's office with backaches and sprains caused by caregiving. To prevent physical injury, remember to lift with your knees instead of your back.

Purchase adaptive equipment for your loved one, such as a walker, a lift chair, or cushions, that will make moving about easier on both of you.

You'll also find a growing line of clothing specifically designed for care recipients that makes bathing and dressing a snap. Spe-

cialized clothing is sold through major department store cata-
logs, such as those from JCPenney and Sears Roebuck.

SEEK OUTSIDE HELP

In addition to the foregoing strategies, seek outside help. The
following are some organizations and agencies you will find in
most communities. (These are discussed in more detail in
upcoming chapters.)

Churches, synagogues, and other religious organizations offer
senior and caregiver ministries. How much they do varies by
locality. Here are some of the more common services offered:

- *In-home respite care for caregivers.* Trained church members
  are paired with caregivers to give them four hours a week
  away from home. In most cases, the service is free, although
  there may be waiting lists.

- *Senior outreach.* This involves special ministries to seniors
  and may provide transportation to religious services in a
  handicapped-accessible van or in a fellow church member's
  car. Special outings to nearby points of interest, shopping
  malls, and the like may be included. Wheelchair-equipped
  vans may be available for doctor appointments.

- *Visitation.* Pastors, ministers, or church members may visit
  with a caregiver or loved one at the person's home.

Another resource is the Caregiver's Program, which provides
publications on caring for the caregiver. Write or call the A. H.
Wilder Foundation, 919 Lafond Ave., St. Paul, MN 55104, (612)
642-2055.

A FEW WORDS ABOUT CAREGIVER ABUSE

This is a touchy subject, but one that needs to be addressed. A
growing number of caregivers suffer physical and mental abuse
at the hands of the very person they are caring for.

Whether it's an alcoholic parent or a loved one with Alzheimer's disease, you should not allow yourself to be abused. Loved ones who drink can become both physically and verbally abusive, affecting your physical and mental health.

If your loved one is an alcoholic, see if you can get the person into Alcoholics Anonymous. If not, join Al-Anon, the support group for people who live with alcoholics. If the situation worsens, seek outside help. Don't ignore it.

You might also need to seek outside help for a person suffering from dementia. Those with Alzheimer's disease, who may not realize what they are doing, often can be helped with medication or by changes in their environment. Talk about such abuses with the loved one's doctor or with a social worker who is well versed in dementia behavior. Don't let it continue, or you'll be the one who is institutionalized.

Part Two

Your financial picture—short and long term

$

It's good of you to look after a loved one and be concerned about his or her finances. But what about your own? Have you been too busy with work, family, and caregiving to think about your financial goals and how you will attain them, as well as about how caregiving is affecting you monetarily? Not paying attention to these areas of your life is *not* so good.

The next half-dozen chapters will ease you into thinking about—and, more important, acting on—savings, estate planning, and other money-related matters. Giving those topics the attention they deserve will help you feel more relaxed about an area of life you *can* have some control over and one that can make you quite pleased indeed over the coming years with financial decisions you make now.

$

CHAPTER SIX

$

How Much Caregiving Can You Afford?

Caregiving is expensive. Even if you are a part-time or occasional caregiver, you're probably spending more money than you realize. It's easy to do.

Think about the little things you buy or pick up for loved ones—not to begrudge the expenditures, but rather to get a snapshot of how much you actually spend.

There's that Sunday dinner out every week with your loved one, because you worry that he or she isn't eating properly. How about all those miles put on the car when you drive your care recipient to the rehabilitation center each week, which costs money for gas and wear and tear on the car? All of this is money spent on caregiving. If you buy adaptive tableware for your care recipient because he or she has arthritis, that's money spent on caregiving. And what about those prescriptions you picked up? Did you pay for them, or did the care recipient? What about the neighborhood kid you paid to cut the grass? It doesn't take much—a few dollars here, a few dollars there—the money adds up.

To help you get a handle on how much you are spending, and on what, take a few minutes to fill out the worksheet in Figure 6.1. Later in this chapter, we'll help you determine how much caregiving you can afford. Subsequent chapters (such as Chapter 8, "Finding Needed Cash") will help you find ways to get money fast, if the need arises.

As you can see, you're probably already spending money on caregiving—perhaps quite a bit. Or you may have found that you can't recall where the money goes!

FIGURE 6.1 CAREGIVER EXPENDITURES FOR A LOVED ONE

EXPENDITURE	DAILY	WEEKLY	MONTHLY	ANNUALLY
Meals at home	$_____	$_____	$_____	$_____
Meals out	$_____	$_____	$_____	$_____
Groceries	$_____	$_____	$_____	$_____
Transportation	$_____	$_____	$_____	$_____
Yard maintenance	$_____	$_____	$_____	$_____
House maintenance	$_____	$_____	$_____	$_____
Custodial care	$_____	$_____	$_____	$_____
Medical care	$_____	$_____	$_____	$_____
Prescription drugs	$_____	$_____	$_____	$_____
Over-the-counter drugs	$_____	$_____	$_____	$_____
Medicare supplement	$_____	$_____	$_____	$_____
Medicare Part B	$_____	$_____	$_____	$_____
Medical equipment	$_____	$_____	$_____	$_____
Adaptive devices	$_____	$_____	$_____	$_____
Rent or mortgage	$_____	$_____	$_____	$_____
Household goods	$_____	$_____	$_____	$_____
Recreation	$_____	$_____	$_____	$_____
Entertainment	$_____	$_____	$_____	$_____
Hobbies	$_____	$_____	$_____	$_____
Total	$_____	$_____	$_____	$_____

▼? DID YOU KNOW . . .
A daily expense log—it need not be more than a small notebook—kept in your car, purse, or pocket can be used to track caregiving expenses as you spend the money.

What is not tallied on this worksheet is time spent caregiving. What if you had to pay someone to perform chores for your loved one? The cost would be much higher. For now, we won't consider your time, but it's something to keep in mind.

————▼▼▼————

Remember that time is money.
Benjamin Franklin (1706–1790)

————▲▲▲————

Now that you know how much money you are spending, how much caregiving can you actually afford? Most of us really don't know.

The best way to answer the question is by looking at your own financial portfolio. We've included worksheets for these as well. Figure 6.2 helps you determine your assets or net worth.

You've probably heard these financial terms before and even may have filled out such forms, perhaps when you applied for your home mortgage or a consumer loan. If not, *net worth* is the difference between what you owe and what you own. The things you own are *assets;* money you owe is a *liability.*

Assets are important because they have long-term value and can be sold, although usually not quickly. Many, such as your home or stocks, will increase in value over the years; others, such as a boat or furniture, could decrease in value over the long run. Assets also can be used to increase your borrowing power or as loan collateral. Chapter 8 contains a more detailed explanation of converting assets to cash.

When you finish, you may wonder what it all means. Where should you stand? It varies, of course. A more appropriate question is, Where do you want to be? If you plan to retire when you're 50, you'll need a lot more money than if you retire at 60 or 70.

FIGURE 6.2 DETERMINE YOUR NET WORTH

ASSETS		LIABILITIES	
Savings account	$_____	Mortgage balance	$_____
Checking account	$_____	Credit card balance	$_____
Savings bonds	$_____	Automobile loan(s)	$_____
Certificates of deposit	$_____	Other secured loan(s)	$_____
Market value of home/condo	$_____	Lines of credit balance	$_____
		Other unsecured loans	$_____
Market value of other real estate	$_____	Other debts	$_____
Cash value of life insurance	$_____		
Surrender value of annuities	$_____		
Equity in pension	$_____		
Value of IRA/Keogh plans	$_____		
Value of stocks/ bonds	$_____		
Value of auto- mobile(s)	$_____		
Resale value of household goods	$_____		
Resale value of furs, jewelry	$_____		
Resale value of collectibles, art	$_____		
Value of boat, other assets	$_____		
Loans due you	$_____		
Other assets	$_____		
Total assets	$_____	**Total liabilities**	$_____

Net worth $_____

(Subtract total liabilities from total assets)

Your retirement plan figures heavily in how much money you can spend for caregiving, because you don't want to shortchange your own future.

Figure 6.3 can help you determine where your money comes from and where it goes. That old platitude, "Easy come, easy go," might come to mind. If you're like most of us, money goes out more easily than it comes in.

When you finish the worksheet in Figure 6.3, you may see that you need to find ways to cut back on daily living expenses—or even increase your income. Some ideas for doing just that follow.

MONEY-SAVING IDEAS

When outlays exceed income or the margin between the two is slim, you have two choices: Increase your income or cut back on spending. If you quit your job or went to part-time status to tend to a loved one, how would you make up the difference in salary?

You may already have a plan. If not, could you start a small business in your home? When one caregiver quit her job to care for her mother who had Alzheimer's disease, she found she needed more money than she previously had thought. Not wanting to leave her mother, she turned her home into an adult day care center. Fortunately, zoning regulations allowed that. She contacted caregivers in her support group and told them she was available to care for their loved ones while they worked. Soon she had four care receivers and had hired someone to help. She enjoyed the work enough to convert her home to a small assisted-living facility specializing in memory-loss patients. Since then, she has built an addition to her home to accommodate three patients whom she cares for full-time and has seven people in the adult day care program. She's making money and caring for her mother and others like her.

> **CAUTION**
> Your state and community may have zoning and licensing rules that prohibit you from converting your home to business use.

FIGURE 6.3 WHERE DOES YOUR MONEY GO?— CASH FLOW

INCOME	ANNUAL AMOUNT
Take-home pay	$
Bonuses	$
Self-employment income	$
Alimony/child support	$
Annual cash gifts from family	$
Net income from rental property	$
Loans due you	$
Interest	$
Dividends	$
Other	$
Total income	**$**

OUTLAYS	ANNUAL AMOUNT
Mortgage or rent	$
Property taxes	$
Alimony/child support	$
Secured loan payments	$
Credit card payments	$
Insurance:	
Health	$
Dental	$
Disability	$
Life	$
Automobile	$
Boat	$
Home	$
Long-term care	$
Utilities	$
Home furnishings	$

FIGURE 6.3 (CONTINUED)

OUTLAYS	ANNUAL AMOUNT
Home improvements	$
Transportation	$
Day care	$
Clothing	$
Laundry/dry cleaning	$
Haircuts/personal care	$
Bills not covered by insurance	$
Education	$
Entertainment	$
Recreation	$
Vacations	$
Gifts	$
Total outlay	$

Surplus/deficit: Subtract outlays from income. The balance is your surplus; if the result is a negative number, you have a deficit.

Of course, that income-generating solution may not work for you. In what other ways can you increase your income? If you've taken on full-time care of a parent who lives in your home, could your parent contribute part of his or her income? Might you reinvest savings or stocks for a higher rate of return? Could you sell your second home if you have one? Chapter 8 will help you with other ideas. If you are unable to find ways to supplement your income, you may have to cut expenditures instead.

CUTTING DAILY EXPENSES

Only you can decide what should be cut from your budget. Look at Figure 6.3 and maybe some ideas will spring to mind. If not, here are some tried-and-true ideas you may not have considered:

- Pay off high-interest credit cards.

- Refinance your house when mortgage rates drop to one to two percentage points below what you are paying (only if you plan to live in your home at least another five years).

- Take in a boarder.

- Combine insurance coverage on your car and home with one insurer if a discount is offered.

- Review insurance policies to determine if you're duplicating coverage (for example, a small boat often is covered under a homeowner policy).

- Form a car pool or take a bus to save on transportation costs.

- Instead of going out to a movie each week, stay at home with a rented video and homemade popcorn.

- Vacation nearby instead of in exotic places.

- Take weekend trips to state and national parks instead of theme parks.

- Save on utility bills: Turn down the thermostat on the hot-water heater and install a timer so that the water heats only when you need it, insulate doors and windows, adjust central heat and air thermostats to their most efficient settings.

▼? DID YOU KNOW . . .
The Energy Efficiency and Renewable Energy Clearinghouse provides free publications on ways to save and conserve home energy. Call (800) 523-2929.

- Make homemade gifts and cards instead of purchasing expensive store-bought ones.

- Cut charitable donations, or donate time instead of money.

As you go through your list, don't feel as though you must cut out everything. Leave enough money for a few leisure activities.

With hard figures in hand, you can now determine how much you can spend on caregiving. Keep in mind that you need to set money aside for your own bills and expenses. The general rule is to have enough money in the bank to cover three months' bills. Money also should be set aside for emergencies, such as car or home repairs, or medical and dental bills not covered by insurance.

If your loved one is willing, complete the same worksheets for his or her expenses to determine how much of the person's money is available for care.

CAREGIVING EXPENSES

What kind of expenses can you expect for caregiving? At the beginning of this chapter, you had a quick look at what you're spending. There are many more expenses and they vary with the individual, but those listed in Figure 6.4 are some common ones. Check off those that apply now, and consider those that may apply in the future. Insurance and Medicare won't cover most of them.

Although caregiving expenses sound costly, you probably will not need all of them, and many are services you or your family can provide. For example, you might do daily and weekly house-cleaning for your loved one and hire someone to come in once a month to do the heavier chores. If your loved one lives with you, do the chores yourself, enlisting help from other family members.

Remember, too, that you or your loved one may qualify financially for the work to be done or the service to be performed by a nonprofit or government agency. A number of agencies have already been mentioned that can steer you to low-cost or free services funded by federal grants under the Older Americans Act or other laws. There's more information on these and other resources in Chapter 13.

You'll learn about meals-on-wheels, a program that delivers hot meals to seniors' homes. Surely, that would cost much less than the meal you may be preparing or purchasing for your loved one now, not to mention the time and gas it takes to deliver lunch. Though a small sum, $3 a day average, 5 days a week, 4

FIGURE 6.4 CAREGIVING EXPENSES

NEED (CHECK)	SERVICE	COST
	Adult day care (Full day, 5 days/week)	$200–$250/week
	Two-week respite care (for your vacation)	$1,500
	Custodial care	$10–$15/hour
	Home-delivered meals	$15/week
	Adult sitter (occasional night out or emergency)	$10–$12/hour
	Lawn care	$20–$50/week (summer)
	Housecleaning	$25–$50/week
	Transportation	Extremely variable, figure $20 per ride average, in a taxi
	Adaptive devices	$5 and up
	Wheelchair ramp	$150
	Bathroom grab bars	$100 with labor

weeks a month, 12 months a year quickly adds up to $720 a year! Now what could you buy with that?

Some things are easier to cut back on. What if you cooked dinner and invited your loved ones to your house, instead of taking them out every Sunday? The savings could be significant: $20 a week for Sunday dinner for two people at a modest restaurant comes to $1,040 a year. You can buy a lot of ham or turkey at that price!

Review your list and think of creative ways you can save money and still provide for loved ones.

Prescriptions are a necessity, but they can be purchased for less. Mail-order prescription houses, such as one offered through the American Association of Retired Persons (AARP),

FIGURE 6.5 HOME CARE ASSISTANCE WORKSHEET

SERVICE	PROGRAM	COST	PAYMENT SOURCE
Example: Caregiver respite	Adult day care	$30/day	Aunt Jan 1 day
Meals Daily	Neighbor Fran (dinner nightly)	$20/week	Dad's income
Weekly	Meals on Wheels free (Lunch Mon.–Fri.)	0	Church
Special	Sunday dinner	$20	Mary and I
Caregiver respite Daily			
Weekly			
Vacations			
Care receiver Socialization			
Home health care			
Transportation Shopping			
Doctor visits			
Pharmacy			
Yardwork/ maintenance			
Housework Light			
Heavy			
Meals Daily			
Weekly			
Special occasion			
Bill paying			
Telephone reassurance			

FIGURE 6.5 (CONTINUED)

SERVICE	PROGRAM	COST	PAYMENT SOURCE
Home safety			
Home security			
Other			

could cut the prescription bill by 20% or more. How about asking your care recipient's physician for samples? Pharmaceutical companies often give doctors free samples of new drugs. Even if the doctor gives you a week's supply, that's money in your pocket. By using a drug's generic equivalent, you can save substantially, sometimes as much as 50%. And if your loved one's income is modest, the Pharmaceutical Research and Manufacturer's Association of America might be able to help. Through its members, this drug company association provides free drugs to indigent, low-income, or uninsured people. Call the toll-free hot line at (800) 762-4636 for a list of programs, qualification criteria, and an application.

One last thought on prescription drugs: Before a new drug is approved for the market, it must pass clinical trials, using humans to prove its effectiveness. People who meet the criteria can volunteer for the trial and receive the drugs free. Often, medical exams are mandatory as part of the testing, and these are free as well. Colleges, universities, and drug research companies are good places to find drug trials. At times, a call for volunteers is placed in daily newspapers.

Go through your list to find creative ways to cut back on some expenses, and brainstorm how you might get services you need at a lower cost. The worksheet in Figure 6.5 will help you do this.

CHAPTER SEVEN

How a Financial Planner Can Help You

Financial planning is a fairly new profession under the huge umbrella of careers in finance. This chapter will help clarify just what these people do and whether you should be one of their clients.

WHY WOULD YOU WANT A PLANNER?

These are busy, confusing times. Over the past several years the stock market has produced huge profits for many. On the other hand, corporate downsizing continues, bringing some employees a cut in salary; others, the far worse loss of a job. The oldest of the huge number of baby boomers are beginning to come into inheritances that many of them do not know how to manage, and newspaper and magazine articles are constantly urging every 40-something worker to begin planning seriously for retirement.

These days the word *money* crops up in thoughts and discussions in just about every area of one's life—work, family, education, leisure, health, and, naturally, finances. Financial planners have stepped in to fill a particular information void that so many

Americans seem to have about money—how to spend it, save it, invest it.

―――――▼▼▼―――――

It can be no dishonor to learn from others
when they speak good sense.
Sophocles (c. 418–414 B.C.)

―――――▲▲▲―――――

You might think you already have a financial advisor: your stockbroker. Does a stockbroker differ from a financial planner, as the term is used today? Yes, it does. Generally, here is how this increasingly active counseling field breaks down.

Stockbrokers can certainly offer financial advice to clients. Indeed, they earn commissions when their clients buy and sell securities through them. Stockbrokers, or *registered representatives,* as they are more formally known, must pass a series of tests and are regulated by both the Securities and Exchange Commission and the National Association of Securities Dealers. Some stockbrokers are also planners, which means that they look at the broader investment and financial picture of their clients.

Someone who is a *registered investment advisor* has also filed credentials and is registered with the SEC. These consultants may recommend stocks, bonds, mutual funds, or any other SEC-registered investment, but there's no test they must pass to be listed by the SEC. Would-be advisors need only fill out a form, which they submit with the required fee. The SEC does not consider registration an endorsement.

Those who call themselves *financial planners* are in a fairly unregulated field. Unlike other professions, there are no uniform standards for planners.

Planners can take a look at your investments and advise you, but they cannot recommend specific stocks and bonds unless they are registered investment advisors (see above). Some are, but some are not. Planners' backgrounds can be quite varied.

Planners must comply with one particular regulation, however: They must file their compensation methods with the SEC. This requirement is helpful to consumers, but, as you might expect, not many potential clients check with the SEC before engaging a planner.

Still, if you choose wisely—and you'll read how to do that later in this chapter—you *can* work with and be helped by a savvy, knowledgeable financial planner. There are many, many of them in this growing field.

GETTING SPECIFIC

What exactly do financial planners do, and how might one help you? Here are a few typical questions these advisors are asked. Do you recognize yourself and your own concerns in one of them? Or maybe some related questions will occur to you as you read what follows.

"I want to retire in 15 years, at age 60, with an annual income of $40,000. How can I do it?"

"I have all my 401(k) assets in my company's stock. Is that good or bad?"

"I just inherited $60,000 from an uncle. How can I best invest it?"

"I'm 34 years old. How do I begin to build an estate?

"I'm 42 and pretty conservative. Should I be a more aggressive investor at this stage of my life, looking for more growth?"

TAKING CARE

As a caregiver, along with your own financial goals, your planning and questions to a planner could include your loved one. You might need guidance about saving and spending for a parent's nursing home care or, if that individual is still at home, for adult day care, or the purchase of needed medical equipment, or any number of other expenses. You might need tax answers as you contribute more and more to your loved one's support.

▼ **DID YOU KNOW . . .**
   A growing number of companies are offering employees financial planning services, and not just the top execu-

tives either. Because the enormous growth in 401(k) savings plans has confused many workers who have invested in them, employees now find themselves looking for guidance in handling them. Maybe yours is one of the workplaces offering this perk.

Planning is the key word in this profession. While other financial consultants may assist you with particular investments—a certified public accountant can, for example, help you with some money decisions and certainly with taxes—a financial planner looks at the broader picture and looks ahead. (However, to make this field even more confusing, sometimes an accountant or a stockbroker also offers his or her services as a financial planner.)

A planner won't put you on a budget. That's not what this is about. But a planner can examine your income and expenses, ask you about your short-term and long-range goals and what's likely to lie ahead for you in income outside a salary, such as a pension, possible inheritance, sale of a home, or maturing of IRAs. You'll need to mention upcoming big-ticket expenses, too, such as college tuition or a child's wedding.

From your profile, the planner can make suggestions that will help you move ahead with your own financial ambitions, while still looking after your care recipient and other family members under your care. The planner's suggestions can cover many areas: insurance, annuities, stocks and bonds, pensions, and other opportunities to generate income for you, either now or in the future. It's a way to have skilled assistance as you carefully ride the rails of those two parallel tracks, saving and spending. Naturally, these are *suggestions;* you are not required to follow them.

Often a planner will refer you to other specialists—an attorney skilled in estate planning, for example, to help you execute a will or a durable power of attorney. A planner might recommend an accountant for answers to tax queries and help with what might be a complicated estate. More on these topics will be presented in later chapters.

SELECTING A PLANNER

If, after reading the foregoing, you believe a planner can help you with your finances, the best way of finding a good professional is the proven one of talking with someone who has done a good job for a friend, a coworker, a neighbor. Your lawyer might also give you a referral.

If asking around does not yield a planner you can work with, check the yellow pages under "Financial Planners." Some of those listed will have initials after their names that denote a membership in a planners' professional association.

You can also call any or all of the financial planning organizations. They will send you information about their particular group and usually some names of member planners in your area. They may offer a "how to choose a financial planner" brochure and even a list of questions to ask a planner.

When it comes to professional associations, you're looking at a somewhat confusing bowl of alphabet soup. There are several groups for planners, each accrediting members with its own set of initials that represents a professional standing for that association. A planner might be "just" a planner or could also be a stockbroker or an accountant, with credentials and memberships in those fields.

Whichever planner you select should be a member of at least one professional association for financial planners. That shows a seriousness of purpose on the part of the individual and a willingness to adhere to a group's professional standards. It also shows that the individual meets the requirements of that particular association and, if it is called for, has passed an exam for certification.

Here are some organizations you can contact for more information on this topic.

- American Institute of Certified Public Accountants offers a personal financial specialist (PFS) designation for members who meet certain criteria. (888) 999-9256; www.aicpa.org
- International Association for Financial Planning. (888) 806-PLAN; www.iafp.org

- Institute of Certified Financial Planners. (800) 282-7526; www.icfp.org
- National Association of Personal Financial Advisors can offer a list of fee-only planners in your area. (888) 333-6659; www.napfa.org
- Securities and Exchange Commission can tell you whether a financial planner is registered with the SEC as an investment advisor. The SEC also provides educational materials on this topic. (800) 732-0330; www.sec.gov
- Certified Financial Planner Board of Standards offers planners the designation CFP after testing and other requirements are met. Some 30,000 planners nationwide hold this designation. To check on a planner you are considering engaging or to lodge a complaint against a planner with this certification, call the board. It also offers a guide to selecting a planner. (888) 237-6275; www.cfp-board.org

—————▼▼▼—————

Life is what happens while you are making other plans . . .
John Lennon (1940–1980)

—————▲▲▲—————

You would be wise to call your city consumer affairs agency to see if a complaint has ever been filed against the individual or firm you are considering. Ask that office which state department or bureau handles grievances against professionals in this field, and call that office, too. And check with the SEC about your planner.

A planner will probably give you a few minutes' free time to see if you are likely to be able to work together. Before heading for that meeting, consider your present financial profile and think about what you need—or want—to accomplish. Read as much as you can about various investments so that you are at least somewhat familiar with the field. Then get your notes together for an in-person interview of 15 minutes or so. Figure 7.1 lists some questions to ask when you interview a financial planner.

**FIGURE 7.1 QUESTIONS TO ASK
A FINANCIAL PLANNER**

- What is your background? How many years have you been in this field? (The longer the planner has been practicing, the better. Try to find someone who has been in practice at least five years.) What did you do before becoming a planner? (That work should have been at least somewhere in the financial arena—accountant, stockbroker, banker, or the like.)

- Do you belong to a professional association? (He or she should be a member of at least one national association for financial planners.)

- Do you have a professional designation? (Ask what initials the planner carries after his or her name. Usually they are given after passing a test or meeting some other qualifications.)

- Tell me about your typical client, in terms of profession and income. (Make certain that you and your needs fit in with the planner's client list. For example, if all of the clients are doctors and you are a college professor, you are likely to be on different saving/spending/investing wavelengths.)

- How many clients do you have? (More than 125 to 150 is too many for one individual to handle adequately.)

- Will you show me a written sample plan that's typical of what you do for your clients?

- What is your fee?

▼ CAUTION
Be wary of the planner who promises you a high rate of return on your investments or who uses pressure tactics to get you to sign up.

Listen to what the planner asks *you*, too. The planner should inquire about your investment plans and goals to get some idea of how far along you are in investing and should be focused on you and your situation. Whether you are a steady saver is important to know, too, as is whether you are extremely cautious or quite aggressive in investing. The planner should be in sync with you, too.

You might be wondering if you have to be wealthy for all of this. Not at all. There are planners interested in clients in every income bracket—even 23-year-olds just starting out in a career (and not making computer whiz kids' salaries).

BILLING STYLES

Naturally, at some point in your interview with a planner you should ask about the charge for the service. The answer will probably be one of three types of fees that planners have adopted.

1. *Commission-based fee.* This isn't the best way to pay. There might be a conflict of interest here because the planner can earn money from selling you what you don't need or particularly want.

2. *Fee-only.* Here you make the same payment no matter what the planner recommends, so any bias on the planner's part is not supposed to be a consideration. If you aren't satisfied, you can simply terminate the arrangement. Presumably, that should keep the planner alert. This is the best method of payment, although not the most common one.

> **▼ CAUTION**
> Fee-only plans may not always be just that. The results of a survey reported in 1997 by the Consumer Federation of America and the National Association of Personal Financial Advisors showed that 58% of all financial planners in the Washington, D.C., area who call themselves "fee-only" are in truth earning commissions and other financial benefits from their clients' investments. NAPFA offers a free booklet, "The Name Game," on how to determine a planner's real compensation method.

3. *Fee-plus-commission.* This is the most common payment method. It includes both a flat rate and commissions for the planner from stocks and mutual funds you purchase. However, you should be free to buy products other than those that the planner and his or her firm are plugging.

Generally speaking, you can expect to pay anywhere from $1,000 to $4,000 for a complete plan—more if you have a complicated financial picture. A common fee is $2,000. That cost should include a written analysis of your financial situation and recommendations of specific investments or investment products. The planner should help you put into effect those recommendations and offer you continual financial advice. (However, as involved as they can get in your life, it's not wise to allow planners to take, or have access to, your assets.)

Whatever payment plan you choose, get that arrangement in writing.

After receiving answers, the smartest decision is to go with the planner that seems right, someone you feel you can trust, and the one with whom you are most comfortable. It boils down to gut instinct. Use yours.

THE SHORT CONSULTATION

You may want to ask a planner only a few questions about your investments, perhaps concerning just one aspect of your financial life. Consider hiring a fee-only planner for just an hour or two. Hourly fees can cover quite a wide range, depending on your location, the experience of the planner, and so forth. Expect to pay from $75 to $250 an hour.

CHAPTER EIGHT

$

Finding Needed Cash

It happens. You're short several hundred dollars for payment of your real estate taxes or a few thousand dollars in tuition for your child.

Perhaps it's money needed to help out a parent—for medical bills or equipment, maybe a mortgage payment or two when you learn your parent has fallen behind.

There are sources of help for you, but before you start seeking that extra cash, keep in mind the following.

1. If it is your care recipient's situation that has caused your financial dilemma, consult Chapter 13 now. It explains the steps you can take to let your loved one stay at home and also includes the names of many community services and programs that can help with expenses. In addition, Chapter 20 lists free products and services for caregivers and recipients.

2. Although you may be tempted to look for an extra job, realistically, it's not an option. With your caregiving demands and perhaps a full-time, or even a part-time, job, plus other family responsibilities, it is not likely you can take on still more work.

3. If you do have a financial advisor, consult him or her to see which solution will work best, given your particular circumstances.

A FEW THOUGHTS ON BORROWING

Whether to borrow to aid an elderly relative you are caring for is not always a clear-cut decision. Medical bills must be paid, of course. Figure 8.1 lists some questions to help you clarify this particular money crisis and better prepare yourself should an emergency occur again.

If the solutions offered in Chapters 13 and 20 won't meet your cash needs, then where *can* you get the money that quickly?

The options that follow are not mentioned in any particular order. Some may be wiser choices than others, but the ultimate selection should be determined by your own financial position.

FIGURE 8.1 SHOULD I BORROW?

- Did this need for cash come out of the blue, or did I see it coming and should have been prepared?

- Is there a way I can work out an arrangement with the creditor, allowing me to repay this amount over time so that I don't have to tap savings?

- If that is not possible, should I cash in savings to meet this obligation?

- Will that leave me dangerously low in the event of another emergency?

- Working the numbers, would it be better for me to leave savings alone and take on new debt in the form of a loan?

- How much should I borrow? Will I have trouble repaying that loan along with other ongoing expenses?

- If it's a withdrawal against an investment, and I don't need to repay that amount, will I still choose to do so?

- Is this particular financial problem likely to happen again?

- How can I see that it doesn't? Can I increase what I now set aside, perhaps with a forced-savings program?

There are no clear-cut answers when you need a sum of money in a hurry. However, addressing these issues will help you examine your present quandary, and all your options, and hopefully steer you toward making some changes for your financial future.

SOME POSSIBILITIES FOR EMERGENCY FUNDS

They are out there. Almost everyone has access to at least one of these possibilities.

CREDIT CARD

A cash advance from one (or more) of your credit cards might solve your problem.

Advantage: You'll probably have the money faster than with any of the other sources.

Disadvantage: You could pay interest on that loan at a rate of 16% to 18%. Interest is higher on a cash advance than it is on purchases made with the credit card. There's a cash advance fee, too.

> **CAUTION**
> "Surfing" credit card companies—going from one to another to take advantage of low-interest introductory offers—can hurt you. Your credit report will list queries from all those lenders. Also, if you leave one card company for another, your balance will be wiped out, but your credit limit might not be, unless you purposely closed that account. Having too much available credit can work against you if you are going to buy a home, refinance an existing place, or borrow for some other reason.

CREDIT UNION

You may find the best credit card rates here, often three or four percentage points below the national average. Credit unions' rates for loans are also below market.

Advantage: Besides those interest rates, there is automatic payroll deduction if you belong to a work-related credit union. Also, most have no cash advance fee, and interest charged is the same as for anything you purchase with the credit card.

Disadvantage: You may not belong to a credit union. If you do, it's important to keep in mind that this is still a loan, no matter how attractive its features. Can you afford a lower paycheck until it is repaid?

HOME EQUITY LOAN

You may be able to take out a home equity loan, based on the amount of money you have in your home free and clear. If your home is worth $150,000, and you owe $75,000 on a mortgage, you have $75,000 in equity.

A home equity loan can be in the form of a line of credit or a second mortgage. Generally speaking, lines of credit are at variable interest rates, while loans for a specific amount carry fixed interest rates. Shop at various lenders for the best terms, the way you would with any loan.

Advantages: With the line of credit you borrow only what you need and you pay interest only on the amount you borrow. With a loan that comes to you in a lump sum, you pay interest on that whole amount.

Another plus: The interest on home equity loans is tax deductible, whereas most other loan programs are considered consumer debt and no tax deductions are allowed.

Disadvantages: You must have enough equity in your home to secure one of these loans. Most lenders will let you borrow from 70% to 80% of your home's current value, less the amount of your outstanding mortgage (some lenders offer more than the value of the house, which can be particularly dangerous if you are already in troubled financial waters). If a lender allows you a 70% loan on a $150,000 home with a $75,000 mortgage, that would be 70% of $75,000, or $53,500.

There can be closing costs with these loans, just as there are with a first mortgage. They can run from 3% to 5% of the amount of the loan, unless you are able to secure some concessions from the lender. Closing costs cover the same charges as they do for a principal mortgage: an appraisal fee, title insurance, possibly points (a point equals 1% of the loan amount), and so forth.

A major disadvantage of a home equity loan is the fact that you will now have both your first mortgage as well as the equity loan borrowed against your house. Falling behind on payments could cost you your home.

A guide to home equity borrowing is available for $3 from HSH Associates, a national mortgage tracking and information service, at 1200 Route 23, Butler, NJ 07405, (800) UPDATES.

Tapping Investments

You may be able to borrow against a life insurance policy. The face value of the policy is, of course, reduced by the amount of the loan. You can make up the borrowed amount by increasing your regular payments. Or you might choose not to repay the money you withdrew.

You might be able to borrow from your pension fund. Most 401(k) plans and some 403(b) funds (they're for nonprofit organizations) allow you to borrow, too—sometimes as much as 50% of your balance. Cashing in certificates of deposit (CDs) and an individual retirement account (IRA) might be another possibility. So is selling stock.

Advantage: With any of these options you are likely to have your money in a few days to a week or so. An intriguing note: When borrowing from some investments, the interest you are charged will, since you are borrowing against yourself, be paid into your own account.

Disadvantage: You are taking money from your savings— money that you might choose not to replace if you aren't forced to. Once it's spent, it's gone. Also, you could be selling investments whose returns have risen quite spectacularly over the last few years, an increase you may not see repeated when you start to save all over again.

Furthermore, cashing in CDs and IRAs prematurely will incur a financial penalty in some cases if you do not pay back the money within a certain time period. You should consult your accountant to see how you will fare taxwise with some of these sales or loans.

SMALLER AMOUNTS IN A HURRY

If you need only a few hundred dollars, you are maxed out on credit cards, and you see no way to come up with even that small amount, there are other alternatives.

Borrowing from the Family

You could ask a relative for a loan. If you need the money to help in your caregiving capacity with a parent, you may well opt for bringing in siblings to help out.

A Pawnshop

Believe it or not, this *could* be another source of cash. Today's pawnshops are not always the dark, cluttered stores they were in the past. Many are now brightly lit, nationwide franchise operations which you wouldn't mind entering to negotiate a deal for your jewelry, television, computer, VCR, or other item of value.

Here's what happens. Suppose you take a ring of some value into the shop (although you could well bring in a number of items at one time). The pawnbroker examines the ring and states a dollar amount the shop is willing to lend you for that item. Although a loan amount can vary from one pawnshop to another, it's usually considerably less than the item is worth, probably one third its value or less. If you accept the pawnbroker's offer, you will be charged from 3% to 25% a month interest, a figure that also varies among lenders. The rate is high but legal. Most loans are due after 30 days, although you may be able to refinance yours for an additional 30 or even perhaps 90 days in all. If you don't repay the loan with interest when it falls due, the broker can sell the item to reclaim the money loaned.

Selling Items of Value

If you don't want to have jewelry, musical instruments, appliances, and the like returned to you the way you would if you pawned them, and if you prefer to receive full value for them (less depreciation), then consider selling goods that could bring you a good price. Having a garage sale is a rather painless way of doing this. You could earn $300 to $500 in a weekend from a sale that was well organized beforehand. That means cleaning and repairing items, pricing them so they will sell, and being willing to negotiate. Getting a few neighbors to have a sale at the same time allows you to advertise a multihousehold sale, which should bring in even more shoppers.

CHANGES FOR THE LONG TERM

Are you looking for an ongoing increase in income, something that lasts longer than a one-time rush?

ROOMMATE? HOUSEMATE? ROOMER?

You can probably guarantee yourself an increased income of a few hundred dollars a month by sharing your house or apartment. This strategy is explained in detail in Chapter 13.

If you don't want that much contact—sharing your whole house or apartment—with whoever is living in your home, consider taking in a roomer. A *roomer* is someone who simply rents a room in your home. The bath can be communal, although a private bath is nice to offer if that's possible and will bring you a higher rent. If you provide your roomer with meals—something you are probably not likely to do, given how busy you are—then the person is a *boarder.*

Check your local newspaper's classified advertisements to see what rooms for rent are going for in your community.

▼▼▼

Money helps, though not as much as
you think when you don't have it.
Louise Erdrich, THE BINGO PALACE *(1994)*

▲▲▲

REVERSE MORTGAGE

Borrowing against the equity in your home as a possible source of income for your parent or other older relative may be appropriate for you. You must be at least 62 years old to qualify for a reverse mortgage. Its good points—it *is* money coming in that you never thought you'd see—and its downside—it can cost you a pretty penny—are detailed in Chapter 13.

THE RIGHT MOVE?

This might be a good time to sell your home and move to a smaller place. Downsizing can bring you a lower monthly mortgage payment, as well as lower all-around housing expenses. Work the numbers, take a look around your present home at what might be wasted space, and you might find it's time to move on. This is a money-*saving* idea rather than a money-*making* one.

CHAPTER NINE

$

You Can Deduct That!

▼▼▼

The state is never so efficient as when it wants money.
Anthony Burgess, YOU'VE HAD YOUR MONEY, 1990.

▲▲▲

ew people enjoy filing an income tax return. Most of us opt for the short form over the long form at every chance. And even though the standard deduction has increased over the years, making it easier to take than itemizing deductions, as a caregiver, you should have your tax filer work the numbers both ways. This is especially important for those caring for loved ones in their homes when the loved ones have little or no income.

The deductions discussed in this chapter are those that most often apply to caregivers and care receivers. Certainly you may have many others that, when combined with these, can make for a sizable tax reduction.

Remember, it's always prudent to consult with a qualified tax professional on your income taxes before you make major financial decisions, as well as when filing income tax forms. You may even want to use a professional who has experience in filing tax returns for caregivers. Check with friends, fellow caregivers, or associations to find one with such experience. We know of several members of a local Alzheimer's association who benefit from the expert tax advice of a certified public accountant who, along with his wife, cares for a father with Alzheimer's disease in their home.

SHOULD I ITEMIZE—OR NOT?

Taxpayers who don't itemize deductions receive a standard deduction. A deduction reduces the income amount on which you are taxed. For 1997 income tax returns, that deduction was $6,900 for a married couple filing together, and $4,150 for a single person. The amount of this deduction usually increases each tax year.

Taxpayers age 65 or older by the end of the tax year and/or who are blind are entitled to additional deductions—if they don't itemize. The deduction can be taken only for the tax filer and spouse. For 1997, the additional deduction is $1,000 for one person filing as single, and $800 for each married person filing jointly. This amount is for each person age 65 or over with an additional like amount for each person who is blind, or who is blind as well as over age 65. Example: A married couple files jointly. Both are 70 years old and one is blind. They receive three additional deductions, or $2,400.

Each filer and his or her dependents also receive an exemption of $2,650 per person, which is given regardless of whether you itemize. However, this per-person exemption is phased out once your adjusted gross income goes above a certain level—in 1997, $181,800 for a married couple filing a joint return, and $121,200 for a single person. Once you reach this threshold, the amount of your exemption is decreased by 2% for each $2,500 increment until it is lost completely.

Figuring exemptions is fairly easy: one for you, one for your spouse, and one for each dependent child who lives with you.

WHO QUALIFIES AS A DEPENDENT?

Under certain circumstances, you may claim an elderly parent as a dependent. To do so, you must meet five criteria. If you meet the test requirements, the person you claim cannot take a personal exemption on his or her own tax return. You may claim a person as a dependent if:

1. The person is a member of your household or a relative. This means the person lived with you for the entire year, except for absences due to illness or if the person was placed in a nursing home for any indefinite period. The person does not have to have lived with you during the year if he or she is related to you in one of these ways: child, grandchild, great-grandchild, stepchild, brother or sister, half brother or half sister, stepbrother or stepsister, parent, grandparent, stepfather or stepmother, brother or sister of your father or mother, son or daughter of your brother or sister, father-in-law, mother-in-law, son-in-law, daughter-in-law, brother-in-law, sister-in-law, or any other direct ancestor.

2. The person is a U.S. citizen. This includes U.S. residents and residents of Canada or Mexico for some part of the calendar year in which the tax year begins.

3. The person does not file a joint return, unless the joint return is a claim for a refund and no tax liability exists for either person on the joint return.

4. The person's taxable gross income is $2,650 or less for the year. The exception is your child under age 19, or under age 24 if he or she is a student. Also note that this rule applies *only* to *taxable gross income;* Social Security payments are not taxable.

5. You provided more than half of that person's total support during the calendar year. To meet this test, add the support you provided and decrease that amount by the person's total income (not just taxable income) that was used for the person's support. Here are two examples from the IRS:

   Example 1: Your mother received $2,400 in Social Security benefits and $300 in interest. She spent $2,000 for lodging and $400 for recreation. Even though your mother received a total of $2,700, she spent only $2,400 for her own support. If you spent more than $2,400 for her support and she did not receive additional income, you have provided more than half of her support.

Example 2: You provide $4,000 toward your mother's support during the year. She has earned income of $600, nontaxable Social Security benefit payments of $4,800, and tax-exempt interest of $200. She uses all $5,600 for her support. You cannot claim an exemption for your mother because the $4,000 you provided is not more than half of her total support of $9,600.

DEFINING SUPPORT

The IRS defines support as food, which means the person's portion of the family food bill if he or she lives in your home; lodging, considered the fair rental value for your area, including utilities, furnishings, upkeep, and depreciation; utilities, meaning that person's portion if he or she lives with you; clothing; education; medical and dental care; recreation; transportation; and other necessities.

> ▼ **DID YOU KNOW . . .**
> You can include the costs of dependent care, such as those for a nurse or adult day care, and still take a deduction for them under Child and Dependent Care Expenses.

If you share the costs of caring for a dependent (such as your mother) with others (such as siblings), only one person can claim the exemption, and only if the aforementioned five-prong test is met.

For example, your mother lives with you and receives 25% of her support from Social Security, 40% from you, 24% from your sister, and 11% from an uncle. Either you or your sister can take the exemption for your mother. Form 2120, or a written statement from the person not taking the exemption, must be attached to the return of the person who takes the exemption.

There are few deductions that caregivers can take over and above those available to all taxpayers. However, Congress has recently recognized the special financial needs of caregivers and authorized new deductions that cover long-term care insurance and expenses and custodial care. More information on this is provided in Chapter 17.

If the person you care for lives in your home, deductions are more plentiful. Some may be taken by the caregiver, even if the care receiver cannot be claimed as a dependent on the care-giver's return. Other credits can be taken by the care receiver if that person has taxable income. In almost every case, with a few exceptions, the Internal Revenue Service allows deductions only for U.S. citizens.

FORMS, FORMS, AND MORE FORMS

If you file your own taxes, you will need additional forms to the 1040 or 1040A. (Most deductions are not available to those who file form 1040EZ.) You can get forms in several ways: by calling, writing, or visiting an IRS office, via a fax-on-demand service, or through the Internet. The IRS has a handy, easy-to-use Web site that explains taxes in plain English. Forms and publications can be read on-line, downloaded into your computer, or printed from the Web site. You can also listen to prerecorded information for over 100 topics on the TeleTax line. Here are some useful Internal Revenue Service numbers:

General information: (800) 829-1040

TeleTax line: (800) 829-4477

Tax forms: (800) 829-3676

Fax on demand: (703) 368-9694

World Wide Web site: www.irs.ustreas.gov

CHILD AND DEPENDENT CARE EXPENSES

If you cared for a loved one during the year, you may be able to deduct up to $2,400 in expenses you paid for the care. In order to qualify, you and/or your spouse must:

- Care for someone who is physically or mentally unable to care for him- or herself (the qualifying person), defined as someone who is unable to dress, clean, or feed him- or herself because of physical or mental problems, or someone who requires constant attention to prevent self-injury or injury to others.

- Have earned income during the year.

- Keep up a home that you live in with the qualifying person. (This means that you and or your spouse paid more than half the cost of running the home for the year; if you lived in the home for less than a year, the cost can be determined on a monthly basis. The qualifying person does not have to live in the home the entire year, if he or she was in the hospital or a nursing home part of the year. The normal costs of keeping up a home include property taxes, mortgage interest or rent, utilities, repairs, insurance, and food. It does not include clothing, education, or medical treatment.

- Pay dependent care expenses so that you and/or your spouse can work or look for work.

- Make payments for dependent care to someone you or your spouse cannot claim as a dependent, for example, for adult day care or for a home health aide or housekeeper if the work includes caring for the qualifying person.

- File as single, head of household, qualifying widow or widower with dependent child, or married filing jointly (with an exemption for a joint return test).

- Identify the person you care for on your tax return (including his or her Social Security number).

If you are reimbursed for care expenses by an employer or government agency, you must deduct the reimbursed amount. There is also a $2,400-per-person exclusion. Your tax credit is then figured as a percentage of your income.

For example, John and Mary pay $150 a week for adult day care for Mary's mother, who has Alzheimer's disease, to enable them both to work. Mary's mother lives with them.

They paid $7,200 for adult day care during the year. Mary works part-time and earns $12,000 a year. John earns $25,000 a year. Here's how the credit is figured.

Adult day care	$7,200
Per-person exclusion	$2,400
Total (whichever is less)	**$2,400**
Mary's income	$12,000
John's income	$25,000
Smallest of the three	**$2,400**
Combined incomes	$37,000

The tax credit is a percentage of the $2,400 based on their combined incomes. It starts at 30% for up to $10,000 in income and ends at 20% for over $28,000. For John and Mary, it is 20%. Their credit is 20% of $2,400, or $480, which reduces the amount of taxes they owe.

MEDICAL AND DENTAL EXPENSES

You may find that some costs associated with providing care for you or your dependents can be deducted as medical and dental expenses, but you must file long form 1040. In addition, you can only deduct expenses that are more than 7½% of your adjusted gross income. For example, if your adjusted gross income is $30,000, 7½% of that is $2,250. If your unreimbursed medical and dental expenses are not more than $2,250, you cannot deduct them.

To claim these deductions, a person qualifies as your dependent, if:

- The person lived with you at the time the expenses were incurred or at the time you paid them.

- The person lived with you the entire year as a member of your household or is related to you.

- The person is a U.S. citizen.

- You provided over half of that person's total support for the calendar year.

Note that you can include the medical and dental expenses of any person who qualifies as your dependent, even if you cannot claim the person as a dependent on your own return. If you cannot take the deductions, perhaps the care receiver can.

Following are some medical and dental expenses that you or your care receiver may deduct:

- Acupuncture.
- Alcoholism treatment center.
- Ambulance service.
- Artificial limbs or teeth.
- Automobile adaptations, including the cost of hand controls and other special equipment installed in a car to accommodate a person with a disability, and modifications to a car or van to hold a wheelchair.
- Birth control pills.
- Books and magazines in Braille.
- Capital expenses, including special equipment you have installed in your home or improvements to your home if their main purpose is medical care for you, your spouse, or your dependent. Note that if the cost of the improvement increases the property value, the deduction is decreased by the resulting new total value. If the value of the property is not increased by the improvement (say, for grab bars in the bathroom or hallways), the entire cost to make the improvement is considered a medical expense. Here are some examples:

  Adding entrance or exit ramps

  Widening doorways at entrances or in the home's interior to accommodate a wheelchair or other devices

  Installing grab rails and support bars

  Lowering or modifying kitchen cabinets or equipment

  Moving or modifying electrical outlets and fixtures

  Installing porch and other lifts

Modifying fire alarms, smoke detectors, and other warning systems

Modifying stairways

Modifying bathrooms

Modifying hardware on doors

Modifying areas in front of entrance and exit doorways

Grading the ground to provide access to the residence

Operation and upkeep on capital assets

- Chiropractor.
- Christian Science practitioners.
- Contact lenses used for medical reasons, including the cost of equipment and materials to clean them.
- Cosmetic surgery that promotes the proper function of the body or prevents illness or disease (no face-lifts!).
- Crutches, cost of purchase or rental.
- Dental treatments, including dentures.
- Diapers and diaper service, when needed to relieve the effects of a particular disease.
- Drug addiction inpatient treatment.
- Eyeglasses (includes cost of examination).
- Guide dog for visually or hearing-impaired people.
- Hearing aids and batteries.
- Home care—maintenance or personal care services provided for qualified long-term care.
- Hospital care.
- Insurance premiums for policies that cover medical care (including HMOs) and Medicare B (but not Medicare A if you are receiving Social Security). Policies can provide payment for hospitalization, surgical fees, etc.; prescription drugs; replacement of lost or damaged contact lenses; or membership in an association that gives cooperative or free-

choice medical services, or group hospitalization and clinical care. Note that self-employed people and certain others may deduct only up to 40% of the cost of health insurance; this rate increases to 45% for 1998 and 1999.

- Laboratory fees not part of your medical care.

- Lead-based paint removal. This deduction is contingent upon having a child in the home who has or has had lead poisoning from eating peeling lead-based paint.

- Learning disabilities treatment—tuition and tutoring fees you pay to a special school or tutor upon a doctor's recommendation, for a child with severe learning disabilities caused by mental or physical impairment.

- Legal fees, limited to those necessary to authorize treatment for mental illness.

- Lifetime care advance payments. You can deduct part of a lifetime care fee or founder's fee paid monthly or as a lump sum to institutions such as continuing care retirement communities. The part paid that is allocated to medical care is deductible; however, the agreement must require a specified fee payment as a condition for the home's promise to provide lifetime care that includes medical care. The deduction also applies to payments for institutions that provide lifetime care, treatment, and training of physically or mentally impaired dependents upon your death, or when you become unable to provide their care.

- Lodging. Deduct the cost of meals and lodging at a hospital or similar institution if your main reason for being there is to receive medical care. The deduction also applies to non-medical institutions (hotels, up to $50 a night), when you are away from home for medical care if:

The lodging is primarily for and essential to medical care.

The medical care is provided by a doctor in a licensed hospital or its equivalent, or a related facility.

The lodging is not lavish or extravagant under the circumstances.

There is no significant element of personal pleasure, recreation, or vacation in the travel away from home.

- Long-term care insurance and expenses. As of January 1, 1997, you can deduct the annual premium of qualified plan policies and unreimbursed expenses for long-term care (see Chapter 17 for information on LTC). The plan is qualified if it's guaranteed renewable, does not assign a cash surrender value, does not provide refunds except upon the death of the insured, and does not pay or reimburse expenses that would be reimbursed under Medicare, unless Medicare is the secondary payer.

- Other expenses required by a chronically ill person, one who has been certified by a licensed health care practitioner within the last year as being unable, for at least 90 days, to perform at least two activities of daily living without substantial assistance from another person.

  This is a welcome tax break for those caring for people with Alzheimer's and Parkinson's diseases, and those who suffer from severe memory impairment.

  Activities of daily living are eating, using the bathroom, transferring from one place to another (such as from bed to chair), bathing, dressing, and continence.

  Also, the person must require substantial supervision to be protected from threats to health and safety because of severe cognitive impairment (such as from Alzheimer's disease).

  The person must also be following a plan of care prescribed by a licensed health practitioner.

  If all these criteria are met, you can deduct diagnostic, preventive, therapeutic, curative, treatment, mitigative, and rehabilitative services, as well as maintenance and personal care costs.

- Nursing home—includes the cost of medical care, food, and lodging in a nursing home or home for the aged, if the main reason for being there is to get medical care.

- Nursing services may be deducted even if they are not performed by a registered nurse, as long as the services are the kind generally performed by a nurse, such as giving medication, changing dressings, bathing, and grooming. The deduction applies whether the services are rendered at home or in a care facility.

If the person also provides personal and household services, these cannot be deducted, unless they qualify under the long-term care provision outlined above.

Remember that you can deduct expenses you pay that enable you to work, as discussed above. If you take deductions for work as well as the nursing services deductions, and the same person performs them all, the deductions must be apportioned. This includes extra rent or utilities paid because you moved to a larger apartment to provide space for the attendant.

- Osteopathy.

- Oxygen, including the cost of oxygen and its equipment to relieve breathing caused by a medical condition.

- Personal items. Certain personal items used primarily to prevent or alleviate a physical or mental defect or illness can be deducted. In most cases, these must be purchased upon the advice of a physician, such as a wig for cancer patients following chemotherapy.

- Prescriptions, including insulin, if prescribed by a doctor. Also, laetrile, where legal.

- Psychiatric care. Deductions are allowed for psychiatric services, including psychoanalysis, psychiatrists and psychologists, and treatment centers.

- Schools, including those for the people who are mentally or physically impaired, for example, teaching Braille to a visually impaired person or lipreading to a hearing-impaired person.

- Telephones, including the cost and repair of special equipment that allows a hearing-impaired person to communicate via a regular telephone.

- Television, including the cost of equipment that displays closed captioning for the hearing impaired and the cost of a specially equipped television that exceeds the cost of an equivalent standard model.

- Therapy, when received as medical treatment.

- Transplants—covers costs of surgery, hospital, laboratory, and transportation expenses for a donor or a possible donor.

- Transportation. When you go to the doctor or the hospital, or for other medically necessary services, you can deduct the cost of a bus, taxi, train, plane, or ambulance, as well as actual car expenses such as gas and oil.

  You can deduct 10¢ a mile for car expenses rather than keeping track of actual expenses. Parking fees and tolls are also deductible. If the person needs the caregiver to go along, the caregiver's transportation is also deductible.

- Wheelchair, mechanical or motorized, used mainly for relief of sickness or disability and the cost of upkeep and operation.

CAUTION
You may have to pay capital gains on medical equipment or property you sell after taking a deduction.

CREDIT FOR THE ELDERLY AND THE DISABLED

This is another deduction that may not apply to you as the caregiver, but may apply to the care receiver. The credit is for people who are age 65 or older by the end of the tax year, or for a person under age 65 who retired on permanent and total disability before reaching mandatory retirement age and who received taxable disability.

If these requirements are met, the person must then meet the income bracket test, shown in Figure 9.1.

FIGURE 9.1 INCOME BRACKET STATUS

FILING STATUS	ADJUSTED GROSS INCOME IS OR IS MORE THAN:	OR	NONTAXABLE SOCIAL SECURITY/PENSION IS OR IS MORE THAN:
Single, head Of household, qualifying widow/ widower with dependent child	$17,500		$5,000
Married, filing joint return, both spouses qualify	$25,500		$7,500
Married, filing joint return, one spouse qualifies	$20,000		$5,000
Married filing separate return, did not live with spouse any time during year	$12,500		$3,750

If income guidelines are met, then a 15% credit, up to $1,125, is given. The credit is derived by a complicated formula. Check with your tax accountant or read Publication 524, Credit for the Elderly or the Disabled, to figure the credit.

STATE TAXES

States that impose income taxes usually allow credits and deductions for people 65 or older, for those who are disabled, and for caregivers. A few states provide extra relief for people caring for loved ones in their homes. Check with your state's income tax division, or contact a competent tax professional.

CHAPTER TEN

$

The Ingredients of a Solid Estate Plan

Where do you keep your will?

Be careful, that's a trick question. If you say, "What will?," then by all means read on—you've given the wrong answer. What follows could be the most important chapter in this book for you.

If your answer is, "At home in a fireproof box," or "My lawyer has it," then you'll want to read the chapter, too, even though you have passed this pop quiz with a gold star. There are other documents that you should be aware of.

All of these papers, plus your investments (more about them in Chapter 11), constitute your *estate plan:* documents you carefully put together for your financial and personal well-being now and for the years ahead. The years ahead include the distribution of your assets the way you want when it comes time to read your will.

Your financial planner can help you in organizing these papers and directing you toward the particular goals you set for yourself. If you don't use a planner, by all means read as much as you can about estate planning, to familiarize yourself with the topic. It is important for every adult to have some of the documents you'll read about in this chapter. It can be especially important for a caregiver. Having your house in order, so to speak, frees you from worrying about the what-ifs when you have so much else on your mind and going on in your life. You know the answer to "What if?" because you have set down your wishes in writing.

Life is complicated these days, with divorce, extended families, single parents, nontraditional households, and the like. Not having written directions, even if you become incapacitated for just a while, can cause consternation and confusion among your family, as relatives try to determine your wishes and perhaps fall far short of what you would have wanted for yourself, for your care recipient, and for others.

As you read this, you might be thinking, "Does Dad have a will?" or "Mom should be doing this. She's 67; I'm only 39." Chapter 18 concerns your loved one's estate and discusses dealing with these documents for that person. This chapter is just for you, the caregiver. You need to look after yourself, too.

You will certainly want a will and a health care power of attorney. Let's take a look at both of these legal instruments.

WHEN YOU DON'T HAVE A WILL

An estimated two thirds of Americans don't have wills. You don't want to be in this group. Dying without a will, or dying *intestate,* as it is legally known, means your assets will be passed on to whoever a judge decides should get them. A judge in probate court must follow certain legal guidelines in determining heirs of intestate estates, but that disposition might not be at all what you would have chosen. For example, your wishes regarding a partner (if you are not married), friends, or charities will not be taken into account.

> **▼ DID YOU KNOW . . .**
> The terms *heir* and *beneficiary* are often used interchangeably by the layperson, but in legal terminology an heir—the deceased's next of kin, whether one person or

several—inherits from an intestate estate. A beneficiary—which can be anyone at all—inherits from someone who dies *testate,* or with a valid will.

In addition, with a will you may save your heirs some money they would otherwise have had to spend to pay state and/or federal estate taxes on your legacy. With advance planning, you may leave a larger estate, too. You would learn which assets do not have to pass through probate.

Do you have minor children? A will also specifies who will be guardian for those youngsters.

Finally, if you have no will, a judge will appoint an administrator to handle your estate until it is closed. That person could be a stranger. And for those duties, he or she will be paid roughly 5% of the estate's worth.

Probate is a special court set up in every state to handle the management of wills, estates of residents who die without wills, and other functions, such as issues of guardianship. Laws governing procedures for probate court vary from one state to another, but its essential function is the same everywhere.

A *probate estate* is all the property and assets of the deceased, distributed under direction of the probate court.

You are likely to hear the buzz phrase, "avoid probate." You may think that it takes a long time to settle an estate that must go through probate court. However, most estates, where there is a will involved and no one challenges it, pass through probate in several months, not a year or two.

Also, you may elect to hold assets in ownership arrangements that can avoid probate altogether, including property owned jointly with another person, life insurance policies and pensions with beneficiaries named, and a living trust, all of which legally skirt the probate procedure.

Another reason for avoiding probate is cost. This is a valid consideration. There is a court filing fee that could run $100 or so (again, each state has its own charge); executor fees of maybe 5% of the estate (unless you name a relative who might take on these responsibilities without pay), and an attorney's fee, which could be another 5% of the estate. Roughly speaking, probate could cost anywhere from 3% to 8% of assets.

> **DID YOU KNOW . . .**
> An *executor* of a will is the person (or perhaps an institution, such as a bank) named to carry out that document's provisions and instructions. The female term (legalese is still behind the times in non-gender-specific wording) is *executrix*.

Certainly if your assets are over $625,000 ($1,250,000 for a married couple), you should seek professional assistance in putting together your will and considering its tax consequences. The first $625,000 of your estate is exempt from taxation. Above that figure, federal estate tax kicks in. That is a levy placed by the federal government on the transfer of property from you to those who inherit from your estate. If $625,000 or less is transferred, there is no estate tax (with some exclusions that your accountant can explain). Also, if you leave all your property outright to your spouse, there is no federal estate tax.

> **DID YOU KNOW . . .**
> You can make a gift of $10,000 to any person during any calendar year and that money is excluded from taxation (the amount will increase after 1998). For example, if you are married and have a child, then you and your spouse can give that child a total of $20,000 in any one year.

Amassing an estate of $625,000 is not all that difficult for many people these days. For example, it's not uncommon for a house to be worth perhaps $250,000 or more. A working farm or ranch might be worth a good deal more. A well-funded retirement plan increases the amount in the kitty. See how it all adds up? Congress also thought it was fairly easy for some of us to build up all that wealth. Thanks to the 1997 Taxpayer Relief Act, the $625,000 exemption rose from the $600,000 it had been since 1988. It'll continue rising in increments each year until it reaches a $1 million exemption, or $2 million for a married couple, in 2006.

Let's get on with drawing up that important document.

THE BASIC WILL

A will does not have to be 10 pages long, containing incomprehensible "whereas" clauses. If your life and your assets are relatively uncomplicated, a simple one- or two-page will might suffice. Keep in mind that everyone of legal age needs a will because every adult has *something* to leave behind, even if that is only personal possessions. There is likely to be a bank account, no matter how small its balance; a car; furnishings; and perhaps some heirloom jewelry or a collection handed down through the family. And what about your pets? Who will care for them if you cannot?

If this sounds like a description of you and your estate, and everything you own is in one state (things get a little more complicated if you own real estate in two or more states), no doubt *you* want to decide who gets those possessions and who will look after your companion animal(s). As already mentioned, in intestate cases a judge assigns your possessions to your legal heirs, who will be your next of kin. You may prefer others to inherit.

You *can* purchase a will form from a stationery store or office supply center (even some supermarkets carry them) and fill in the blanks. You can also buy computer software to help you write one.

Neither of these options is the wisest way to go. For one thing, each state has its own requirements for a valid will, and you might not notice those particular paragraphs or, indeed, they may not be included in the do-it-yourself package you purchase. Naturally, a lawyer *will* know what's what in your state. Also, having a will drawn up by a lawyer will give you an opportunity to ask questions about your estate. You might want to know, for example, if you are holding assets in an ownership style that will help you avoid probate and its costs, how you can save on estate taxes by making gifts now rather than through your will, and other strategies of financial benefit to your estate and your loved ones. Perhaps your attorney will refer you to an accountant for specialized advice. That will be money well spent, too. Figure 10.1 will help you prepare for drawing up a will.

To have a will drawn up, you can expect to pay a lawyer from around $100 to $400 or more for a complicated estate. That's a relatively small amount of money for purchasing peace of mind.

There are suggestions for finding a lawyer at the end of the chapter.

FIGURE 10.1 BEFORE HAVING YOUR WILL DRAWN UP

Besides listing your assets for your will, you will need to know *how* you own them. For example, most married couples own property as "joint owners with right of survivorship," which means that at the death of one, the deceased's half of the property automatically goes to the surviving spouse. You can't will a jointly owned asset to anyone else.

Or perhaps you own property as "tenants in common," which means that those owners can bequeath their share of that asset to anyone they choose. Another possibility as you go through your files is that you might have already named specific beneficiaries for an insurance policy and/or pension plan.

When you have the necessary papers collected or notes jotted down, this worksheet will help you prepare for having your will drawn up. You can take this sheet with you to a lawyer.

ASSET	DOES ANYONE AUTOMATICALLY INHERIT? HAVE I NAMED A BENEFICIARY ON THAT DOCUMENT?	IF ANSWER IS NO TO BOTH THOSE QUESTIONS, I'LL LEAVE IT TO:

Specifically about Caregiving

If you are a primary caregiver, you absolutely should see a lawyer about preparing a will.

If you and your care recipient have limited resources and you fear for the person's well-being should you predecease him or her, you should know that Medicaid will probably step in and provide nursing home care for the person. Medicaid (in California it's known as Medi-Cal) is a state-run plan with federal funding that provides certain minimum medical benefits to persons who qualify financially (there is a fuller discussion about Medicaid in Chapter 16). Each state has its own rules about who qualifies. Recipients primarily are aged, blind, or disabled people who are eligible for supplemental Social Security and those eligible for Aid to Families with Dependent Children.

You will be interested to know that about 40% of all nursing home bills are paid by Medicaid.

However, you may want to think twice about remembering a loved one in your will. As far as your estate is concerned, you could cancel that relative's eligibility for Medicaid by bequeathing the person some of your assets. If the person's eligibility is not cancelled, it might be delayed.

Medicaid is for those who need financial assistance. There are more than a few applicants who divest themselves of most of their estates by making gifts to family members and then calling on Medicaid to look after them. That strategy hasn't slipped by the government. Congress imposes a penalty for assets owned and then transferred by a Medicaid applicant within 36 months of that individual's accepting Medicaid. If your parent inherits from you, it throws a monkey wrench into that time frame, and could possibly extend the 36-month look-back period to five years (see Chapter 16).

Keep in mind, too, there is no *financial* obligation on your part to look after your care recipient. You may certainly feel a moral or ethical obligation to do so, but you are not required by law to support a relative.

DID YOU KNOW . . .
   If you have a lawyer draw up a will for you, ask him or her about a health care power of attorney at the same time. You might save money by not being billed for two separate visits.

A HEALTH CARE POWER OF ATTORNEY

This document, which can also be known as a health care *proxy*, is another must-have for your estate file.

It provides that an individual named by you is authorized to make medical decisions for you when you are not capable of doing so. It is especially important for you to have this form if you have no close relatives (and your care recipient, although perhaps closely related, is not able to act in your behalf).

The health care power of attorney makes your wishes very clear—especially if you would prefer certain family members over others, or perhaps someone outside the family, to speak for you in the event that you cannot do so.

You (known as the *principal*) choose the agent to act for you. If at some time in the future you want, let's say, artificial life support measures terminated if you are seriously ill, then the person with your health care power of attorney acknowledges your wishes and passes them on to the appropriate medical authorities to be implemented.

There is more to it than that, of course. A principal can also ask that the agent request an autopsy, admit or release him or her from health care facilities, make anatomical gifts on the principal's behalf, and even plan for the disposition of the principal's body.

Naturally, you will review all the power of attorney's provisions with the agent you choose to make certain the agent understands exactly what your wishes are and will convey them if the time comes. It would be wise to have a secondary proxy named in the event that your primary agent becomes incapacitated or loses touch with you over the years.

DID YOU KNOW . . .
A durable power of attorney, a health care proxy, and a living will are all frequently referred to as *advance directives.*

Talk about your preferences in this area with your family, too, so that they know how you feel about the subject.

You'll be smart to seek an attorney's guidance here; requirements for a valid form differ among states.

A LIVING WILL

You might decide on a living will instead of a health care power of attorney. These have become quite popular in recent years. Is there a difference between the two? Yes, an obvious one and one that's fairly subtle.

The health care power of attorney is a legal instrument that names an agent to make health care decisions for you if you become incapacitated. In contrast, a living will simply authorizes someone to tell doctors to take you off life support systems.

Also, as valuable as living wills can be, they can be ignored by personnel at hospitals, rehabilitation centers, nursing homes, and other such institutions. Sometimes a medical staff is reluctant to take such drastic wishes into account. However, the health care power of attorney—if you have drawn up such a document to go along with the living will or instead of it—is not easy to ignore, although it has on occasion been set aside, too.

You can ask your lawyer about both documents, although you do not need a lawyer if you opt for just a living will. You might call large hospitals or medical centers, which often supply living will forms. Stay within your state, though, because there are regional differences among these documents. Although some states have reciprocity laws that permit a properly executed living will from another state to be valid there, it's just as easy—and wiser—to request a form from your own state.

▼ **CAUTION**
Not all health care power of attorney forms mention organ donation and, depending on the situation, there may be no time to look for that document. If you want to be an organ donor, contact a hospital near you. Many health care facilities have donor cards that they send to area residents at no charge. You can also call the United Network for Organ Sharing (UNOS) at (800) 24DONOR. They will send you several cards at no cost to you. You should carry your donor card with you at all times.

You must remember that your witnesses to these forms should not be members of your family or anyone who has any financial stake in your death—your beneficiaries, for example. The reason for this is the possibility that the documents could be signed under duress from a possible inheritor.

These are the two most important documents you can draw up right now, but there are others you may eventually want or need.

MAYBE A TRUST?

Certainly having a will is good, but you might find you'll be better off financially and will have your wishes followed more exactly if you also institute a trust. Trusts have been around for centuries, but have become increasingly popular just in the last several years.

There are two types of trusts. A *testamentary* trust is established in a will and becomes effective when the will is probated. It is not a separate document. This trust takes your assets and transfers them to the trustee, as if that individual were the beneficiary of the will. The trust survives probate and goes on for as many years as you have designated, carrying out your wishes as noted in it. In contrast, a will is concluded and its assets distributed after probate proceedings.

The problem with a testamentary trust is that your assets *do* have to go through probate. If your goal is to avoid that, then the wiser move is to set up a *living* trust.

A living trust is a written arrangement in which you (known as the *grantor* or *trustor*) transfer property during your lifetime to another party (known as the *trustee*), to hold for the benefit of a beneficiary. At your death, your assets are distributed to those beneficiaries, according to the terms of the trust.

You can elect an *irrevocable* living trust, but that is not as popular as the *revocable* living trust because, once an irrevocable living trust is established, it is impossible to revise. Its terms are indeed *irrevocable*.

The benefits of a revocable living trust are as follows:

- You can sell, spend, or give away your assets while you are still alive. You can change the trust, or cancel it, any time before you die.

- Unlike a will, which is untouched until your death, certain trust funds can be invested during the life of the trust, so your assets can grow.

- You can serve as your own trustee (but it's wise to name a successor trustee in case you eventually are not capable of acting in that role, and, too, if you want the trust to continue for some time after your death).

- Assets in the trust pass to the trust beneficiaries outside of probate and can go on for as many years into the future as you designate. There is no time wasted in probate and no probate expense.

- While disgruntled relatives may contest a will, a revocable living trust is more difficult to challenge.

- You can avoid court-appointed guardianship if one is needed someday. A co-trustee or successor trustee can take on that job.

- A trust is private, whereas a will, when it is filed, is a public document allowing anyone access to its contents.

? DID YOU KNOW . . .
A testamentary *special needs trust* (sometimes called a *supplemental needs trust*) set up by you can allow your loved

one who is a Medicaid recipient to pay for private nurses, experimental drug therapy, and other expenses Medicaid does not allow. Check with your lawyer.

Is there a downside to a living trust? It does not have any special tax advantages (although there are some complex versions of the simple trust that help married couples avoid some or all estate taxes). Also, a trust does require a lot of record keeping and updating, since you must keep your estate current, filing receipts, deeds, and the like. (You may choose to keep some items outside the trust. Your car might be one, if you do not want to report to the trust every sale, purchase, and repair.)

Also, since most trusts are *not* supervised by a court, there is always a danger of misappropriation. So you must be sure you trust your trustee if it is not yourself or your spouse. Trust your successor trustee, too. You might request an accounting of the trust to its beneficiaries each year. Have the trustee take out a bond, too, to protect you from wrongdoing.

If you select an institution as trustee—the trust department of a bank, for example—be sure to interview a few banks before making a decision. Inquire about their fees (usually about 5% of the trust assets), and ask about their policies and who will be investing your assets. Look for continuity, too: Be sure you will be dealing with one particular trust officer.

State laws vary about trusts and certainly trust laws are complex. If you want to do it yourself, be certain that the document complies with the laws of your state. Otherwise, it could be declared invalid. A better option is to see a lawyer.

WHO SHOULD USE A TRUST?

People who have minor children might want a trust for those youngsters in the event that the parents die simultaneously. A lifelong trust is beneficial for the special-needs child of any age. And many of us have heard of the "spendthrift" trust, which gives money in stages to children or young adults who parents think cannot handle a one-time windfall.

A revocable living trust can work well for those who are married and have children from a previous union. Some retirees prefer a trust to manage their funds so they do not have to bother with that aspect of their lives. The trust can also handle their affairs when they are no longer able to do so. Also, a trust can, of course, be important for those who have estates totaling more than $625,000.

However, if you are a young single person, or a young married couple just starting out, you are not likely to need a living trust. It will cost more to have one drawn up—$1,000 to $1,500—than a will does, too. This is not as simple, or as inexpensive, a document as a will, which makes those who truly do not need one think twice about the idea.

If you have a living trust, you will probably need a will along with that document to cover assets you have not listed in the trust. A will is also necessary to name a guardian for your minor children.

A DURABLE POWER OF ATTORNEY

This is another document you eventually should add to your estate file.

A durable power of attorney authorizes someone to act on your behalf if you are not able to act for yourself. This legal instrument continues to be valid if you become incapacitated. In fact, it can be dissolved only when you choose or when you die.

The durable power of attorney can list many functions and powers that the chosen individual will take on, including paying bills for you, filing tax forms, and handling your investments. In fact, the form can grant power to do almost anything you choose.

It has this benefit as well: If you become incompetent and have no durable power of attorney, then a guardianship may be required, which means that a close family member will have to petition a state court to be appointed your guardian. This can be expensive (court filing fees, attorney fees), and although it is *likely* a court will appoint that family member, it is not a certainty.

And what if the court-appointed guardian is a family member you would *not* have chosen? (Chapter 18 contains more information about guardianship.)

To avoid having a guardianship by default, you have the choice of the durable power of attorney or a living trust.

Naturally, if you elect to have a durable power of attorney, you will name someone you trust completely—an absolute necessity since that individual's powers are likely to be extensive.

This is also a job for a lawyer. State requirements for valid documents are likely to vary.

> **CAUTION**
> Over the past several years, states have enacted specific laws creating *durable* powers of attorney, which could mean that an older form designated simply "power of attorney" may not include the "durable" authority and should be reexecuted. Be sure any new form you sign has the word *durable* in the title.

Some durable powers of attorney contain clauses relating to health care, but most do not. To cover health-related issues, you're likely to need the health care proxy previously discussed in this chapter.

CHOOSING A LAWYER

Where can you find a lawyer? The best reference is always a satisfied customer. Ask family, friends, and coworkers if they can suggest anyone.

Since you want someone skilled in estate planning, you might also call The American College of Trust and Estate Counsel, at (310) 398-1888, for a list of estate planning attorneys in your area, or reach them on the Internet at www.actec.org.

If you are near or past retirement age, you will find an elder law attorney particularly helpful in drawing up these documents. Refer to Chapter 1 for guidance in finding a lawyer with this specialty in your area.

IS PREPAYING YOUR FUNERAL WISE?

You might be too young to have considered paying for your funeral ahead of time. This expenditure usually occurs to retirees. For that reason, there is a discussion of prepayment in Chapter 18. However, the bottom line on the subject of paying ahead is: Don't.

WHERE TO KEEP ESTATE PAPERS

Your will, trust papers, durable power of attorney, and other important documents should be kept in a fireproof box at home. Your lawyer or your physician will keep the original of some of these documents. Be careful about leaving the original of any document in a bank's safe deposit box. In some states safe deposit boxes become frozen at the renter's death until their contents can be examined for taxation purposes. You certainly want your will to be easily accessible to your family, especially if it contains funeral instructions.

Leave a letter of directions, telling your next of kin where all of these papers and any other important financial records can be found. You might need to list addresses and telephone numbers as well.

> **CAUTION**
> Safe deposit boxes in a bank are not insured by the Federal Deposit Insurance Corporation (FDIC) the way your savings are with those institutions. In the event of a theft or fire at your bank, what you have in that box may be gone forever. Neither catastrophe is likely to befall you, but keep the possibility in mind when storing irreplaceable items or the original of any documents.

YOU'VE DONE IT!—FOR NOW

Congratulations. If you have implemented the suggestions in this chapter, you have, unlike many others, taken the bull by the horns and got your estate documents in order.

FIGURE 10.2 WHEN TO RECHECK YOUR WILL (AND POSSIBLY OTHER ESTATE DOCUMENTS)

- When your family changes, as a result of marriage, birth, adoption, divorce, or death. Also, when children reach adulthood and are no longer dependents.
- When new estate tax laws are enacted.
- When you start up or close down a business.
- When you move to a different state. (You may need to alter your will, since laws vary from state to state.)
- When you buy property in another state. (It may be subject to the laws of that state, rather than the state where you live now.)
- When an inheritance or other event boosts your assets substantially, so that you now have more to bequeath in your will.

Still, you cannot "file 'em and forget 'em." You should pull out your file at least once a year and review those papers. Do they still represent your wishes? Is your family situation different now?

Figure 10.2 lists examples of important changes in your life or outside forces that should prompt you to review your estate papers.

CHAPTER ELEVEN

$

And What about Your Savings?

All the talk of money in the last several chapters didn't mention the business of saving it.

You may have been so busy over the last few years with caregiving and other responsibilities, which may include a full-time job, that you haven't given much thought to savings. Even if you are putting a little aside from your paycheck, you may not have a *plan*.

There is a better way that can save you many tense moments worrying about money. You need to manipulate your savings and investments a bit differently to bring you more return. Doing that can make retirement look financially rosier, too. You can talk to an accountant or financial planner for advice about getting the maximum return from savings, at the least cost to you in taxes.

Take a close look at what and how you are saving, make some needed changes, and you can breathe a little easier about *that* aspect of your life.

THE IMPORTANCE OF LIFE INSURANCE

If you are younger than the senior you are caring for, then you need life insurance. (If you are over 65, you may not need to keep paying on a policy, as you will read in Chapter 17.)

Why is this is a necessary ingredient in a saving plan?

- Life insurance can benefit your family enormously if some-thing should happen to you. This is especially important if you have minor children or older kids to put through col-lege, and a spouse who would like to be able to remain in your present home. That money will be available to your beneficiary immediately after your death, too, unlike some assets that wouldn't be distributed immediately.

- If you are single, life insurance is important for you, too. It can provide immediate cash for funeral expenses, payment of credit card bills, and other debts that would otherwise have to be paid by your estate before your assets go to your beneficiaries.

- Whole life insurance, which you will read about later in this chapter, can serve as a savings account for you.

- Life insurance will go to the one you designate, with no income tax bill attached.

Overall, life insurance can significantly increase your estate, and at not that great an expense to you.

INSURANCE CHOICES

You have a couple of life insurance options, and even choices within those selections.

Term life insurance is simple life insurance and offers you the best deal for its cost (premium rates depend on a number of fac-tors, including your age). You can select a $100,000 (or less) pol-icy, or one for $500,000 or much more. You pay an annual premium, and if you die while owning the policy, your benefi-ciary receives the value of the policy. You can't borrow against this type of coverage, though, because there is no cash value.

Cash value life insurance, sometimes called *whole life insurance,* often has a savings feature included in the policy and a borrow-ing one, too. There are several varieties of cash value coverage, which you can discuss with your financial advisor or an insurance agent.

How Much Insurance?

You need to purchase enough insurance to meet the needs of your family, at a premium rate you can afford. If you are married, consider how much money your spouse will need to meet current expenses without having to change drastically his or her standard of living. Incidentally, if you and your spouse both work, you both should be insured. Look at it this way: If the absence of one income will be felt in your two-income household, then both working people should carry insurance.

If your employer carries group term life insurance policies for employees, why not sign up for that along with your personal policy? There are some tax advantages to group insurance from the workplace.

Beneficiaries

This could be an easy decision for you. A spouse is likely to be the beneficiary and children the alternate beneficiaries. If you have minor children, you might prefer to establish a trust for them to receive the insurance proceeds and then manage those assets until they become older.

> **CAUTION**
> You'll want to review your beneficiary designation periodically, certainly if there is a change in your life situation, such as marriage, divorce, or death in your immediate family. Be sure to name an alternate beneficiary, too, in the event that the beneficiary dies before you do. If you have no alternate listed, the insurance proceeds go into your probate estate.

For More Information

You are bound to have more questions about insurance that are beyond the scope of this book. Also, everyone's insurance needs and qualifications for policies are different.

For answers to questions, you can contact the National Insurance Consumer Hotline at (800) 942-4242. This service is sponsored by several insurance industry trade associations (it also covers home and auto insurance). The hotline is in operation weekdays from 8 A.M. to 8 P.M. EST.

"What You Should Know about Buying Life Insurance" is a brochure offered by the American Council of Life Insurance, a trade association of 600 life insurance companies. Call (800) 338-4471.

ABOUT ANNUITIES

Whether through your workplace or on your own, you can put as much money as you like each year into an *annuity*. This is an investment vehicle that brings a fixed, periodic return for a specific number of years (or a lifetime or, if you wish, the lifetime of your spouse). Unlike some investment vehicles, you can put as much as you want each year into an annuity. Your money grows without taxation, too. But the amount you deposit is *not* deducted from the earnings you report.

> ▼ **DID YOU KNOW . . .**
> If you're saving for retirement, the big advantage of an annuity is deferring payment of income earned until then, when your tax rate is likely to be lower than it is now. You might ask an accountant or financial planner about other investments to bring you returns, or at least the bulk of those payments, after you retire so that you pay less in taxes on them.

Annuities can be purchased through insurance and some mutual fund companies. They are quite safe, though with limited returns. A riskier investment is the *variable annuity*, which allows you to choose a portfolio from among stocks, bonds, and money market instruments. The value of your annuity then is tied to the investments you choose and to the ups and downs of the market. Talk to your accountant or planner about the wisdom of this type of purchase and the type of annuity that is likely to work best for you.

DISABILITY INSURANCE

This insurance coverage can be a must in many situations.

If you just can't afford an illness that keeps you from work and the subsequent loss of income, whether for a short or long period of time, then you need disability insurance.

Interestingly, fewer than 40% of workers carry this coverage, virtually all of them signing up for it where they work. The reason for the low numbers: It *is* pricey. You can expect to pay annual premiums of about 2% of your gross annual income. So if you earn $60,000, that's $1,200 a year.

Is there any way around these costs? If not, how do you at least get the best coverage?

- You can certainly look into disability insurance at your workplace, where you might have a group policy offering a better rate than one person buying alone could be offered. If your company's policy does not offer enough coverage for you, you can add to it on your own.

- Look for an *income replacement policy,* not one that pays you if you cannot work at your specific job. It's broader.

- Choose a long waiting period before benefits kick in. That'll cost you less, and you may be able to get along just fine with your own funds for 60 or 90 days before receiving a disability check.

- See what your company has to offer, but shop around, too. You may find better rates and benefits with another carrier, since each has its own rates and benefits. If you keep extras to a minimum—cost-of-living increases, for instance—you'll pay less in premiums.

WILL YOU HAVE A COMPANY PENSION?

A pension plan can also be a forced savings plan for you now, allowing you to determine what your pension check might be.

WHICH TYPE OF PLAN?

You can have a *defined-benefit pension* where you work, whereby the amount an employee will receive at retirement is fixed—say, $2,000 a month. That sum is determined by years of service and average compensation of the employee during that time, based on a formula built into the plan. The employer is supposed to allot enough money to fund these benefits, using actuarial calculations of how long the employee (and spouse, if married) is expected to live. The employee contributes nothing to this plan. Aside from a few variables, it is a clear-cut benefit, allowing you to know for certain the amount you can expect in a pension check when you retire.

With a *defined-contribution pension,* benefits are based on the amount that is contributed by the employer and the employee and that accumulated income. These plans can have different names. Some of the most common are 401(k) programs or 403(b) for those who work for not-for-profit companies. With this type of pension, each plan participant will have a different account balance. What participants receive at pension time is not a fixed amount, but rather the amount of money they have put into the plan before retirement. Each will likely invest a certain percent of his or her salary, which can be matched by the employer.

Incidentally, you start paying taxes on pension money when you begin receiving those retirement checks.

LEARNING MORE ABOUT *YOUR* PENSION

Pensions are protected under several federal laws, among them the Employment Retirement Income Security Act (ERISA), the Retirement Equity Act (REA), and the federal Comprehensive Omnibus Budget Reconciliation Act (COBRA). Protection is limited, though, because a pension is still a contract between an employer and employee, with minimum requirements set by law.

The rules that govern pension plans spell out the type of plan, such as who qualifies and when; employee earnings; and what happens when an employee leaves that company. Since most companies contribute something to employees' pension plans, laws also dictate when the company's contributions become the employee's, called *vested rights*. *Vested* means the money is yours; it cannot be taken away from you.

In 1989 ERISA provided that an employee be vested 100% after 5 years of employment in a company or that an employee be vested a specified percentage after 3 years, with the remaining percentage apportioned each subsequent year. For some union-negotiated multiemployer plans, an employee must be 100 percent vested after 10 years.

Remember, when considering your financial future, that a spouse's vested pension, at a rate of at least 50%, becomes yours if he or she should die, unless you have previously signed away that right.

▼ CAUTION

If you're leaving your company, seek advice from an accountant about your 401(k) and how leaving it or taking it with you will affect your taxes.

For answers about your employee plan, you can contact the Pension Rights Center, 918 16th Street NW, Suite 704, Washington, DC 20006, (202) 296-3776 (the center has no Web site).

"Your Guaranteed Pension" answers frequently asked questions about private pension plans. The brochure is free from the Consumer Information Center, Department 521E, Pueblo, CO 81009.

Finally, to look into what's due you from your own pension, you'll find some guidance in the checklist in Figure 11.1.

CREATING YOUR OWN PENSION FUND

If your company does not offer a retirement plan, you can fund your own pension with an *individual retirement account* (IRA). This is an interest-earning account you set up yourself through any bank, credit union, or investment company, and to which you contribute money. Contributions for any calendar year can be made until April 15 of the next year.

FIGURE 11.1 PROTECTING YOUR PENSION RIGHTS

The U.S. Department of Labor Pension and Welfare Benefits Administration (PWBA) offers these suggestions for protecting your pension rights:

✔ Keep a copy of your plan description, which outlines its benefits and provisions.

✔ Periodically obtain, and then review, your individual benefit statement that documents your work history.

✔ Inform your pension office of any change in your status: marriage, remarriage, divorce, or death of a spouse.

✔ Notify your pension office of your address if you change jobs.

The PWBA answers questions about pensions and gives employees advice about pension problems. You can call its advisors at (202) 219-8776.

To qualify, you must be under 70½ years of age and you or your spouse must have received taxable compensation during the year you contribute to the IRA. You may not make contributions during years in which neither you nor your spouse receives taxable compensation. So if you are single and leave your job (to take on full-time caregiving, for example), and you have no taxable income that year, you cannot take a deduction for that year. On the other hand, if you have a spouse who continues to work after you have resigned from your job, both of you can make contributions for that year.

A married couple filing a joint tax return can each contribute up to $2,000 to an IRA each year. A single person can also contribute as much as $2,000 annually. Full tax deductions have varied income caps for investors, but these caps have increased as a result of the Taxpayers Relief Act of 1997.

Interest earned on an IRA is taxed, but not until you begin withdrawing money.

With some exceptions you cannot make withdrawals from your IRA until you reach age 59½. Should you need to make a withdrawal before that age, you will be penalized 10% of the amount you take out. You will also have to claim the amount you withdrew as income on your federal tax return for that year.

Cashing in your IRA early does not *always* cost money: The law now allows IRA withdrawals without penalty if the money is used to buy a first home, pay higher education expenses, or pay major medical bills.

▼ **DID YOU KNOW . . .**
If you must withdraw money from your IRA for an emergency, you will not be penalized at all if you replace that amount within 30 days.

Also, you can take out your IRA penalty free if you withdraw it in approximately equal annual amounts that will exhaust the account over your life expectancy. For example, if you are 50, and your life expectancy is 72 (according to IRS actuarial tables), you can take your money with no cost to you in equal install-ments over 22 years. So if you had $22,000 in your IRA, that would amount to $1,000 a year over those 22 years.

ROTH IRA

As part of the 1997 tax changes, Congress authorized a new sav-ings vehicle called a Roth IRA. While in many ways similar to the traditional IRA, it has key differences: Unlike traditional IRAs, contributions to Roth accounts are not tax deductible. Instead, earnings from a Roth IRA are not taxed when they are with-drawn, so long as the saver keeps the account for at least five years and doesn't tap it until he or she is 59½. With the Roth IRA, contributions are permitted after age 70½ if the saver has earned income, and there is no requirement to begin taking distribu-tions when you reach 70½.

The Roth and traditional IRAs are complex strategies that you may want to discuss with your accountant. If you're on-line, you can also check:

- www.rothira.com   This site has lots of information—legisla-tion text, articles, and the like—exclusively about the Roth IRA.

- www.irs.ustreas.gov/plain/hot/tax-law.html   Provided by the Digital Daily Special Report (Internal Revenue Service), this provides an overview of the 1997 Taxpayers Relief Act, including, of course, an explanation of the Roth IRA.

You can, if you choose, have both a traditional IRA and a Roth IRA, provided your annual contributions do not exceed the maximum allowed. For example, if you file as a single person, you can contribute $1,000 to the IRA and $1,000 to the Roth IRA. A traditional IRA can be changed to a Roth, if guidelines for rolling over IRAs are followed.

An educational IRA is another new variation on the traditional individual retirement account. It can go toward school costs for a child (who does not have to be your own) under age 18.

KEOGH PLAN

If you are self-employed, you probably know you can receive qualified retirement benefits under this plan, which covers sole proprietors and partners and can include employees. Your savings with this plan and taxability after you begin receiving that money in retirement are similar to defined-benefit or defined-contribution pension plans, depending on which form is used in the Keogh plan. You should seek legal and tax help to set up one of these.

NON–WORK-RELATED SAVINGS

From a bank savings account to stocks, bonds, and mutual funds to gold bars, there are any manner of other investments to help you financially over the next several years and certainly to become a welcome addition to a comfortable retirement. You might have the ability to put more money aside now, while you are working, than you will after you retire. Take advantage of that opportunity! Remember, investments need several years to grow.

Important to your immediate needs now is having an emergency fund. An old adage says one should have enough money saved to pay three months of bills and other expenses. For larger sums—say a year's worth of bill paying—you might have certificates of deposit (CDs), which provide a (slightly) higher yield than a savings account. If you can, purchase them to mature at staggered dates, so there is always another one coming due in the event that you need money unexpectedly.

Look at some of your savings for that *liquidity*. That is the ability to convert paper into cash as quickly as possible. Stocks and mutual funds are liquid, bringing you your money within days of selling. CDs are a pretty fast pay, too, but they carry penalties for premature withdrawal. To take another example, your house, while a quite sizable investment, is not liquid at all. It would take weeks—more likely, months—to have cash in hand from that sale.

THE GROWING POPULARITY OF INVESTMENT CLUBS

You may have read about these groups of everyday people getting together for the purpose of making money. They invest in stocks and/or mutual funds, each contributing money and research on companies in which to invest, and then sharing profits.

You might want to see if there is an investment club in your area that you can join. Perhaps it would be possible for you to slip out one night a month to attend meetings, or maybe you could have the club meet at your home. This isn't a costly business. With most clubs, members pay only $20 to $50 a month into the group pool, which is used for stock purchases.

Along with the moneymaking aspect of the club, it's a good opportunity for socializing, too. You might be long overdue for getting out a bit and not thinking about caregiving for a few hours.

If you can't find an investment club, and you have the time, you might want to consider starting one with three or four like-minded friends. You can purchase *Starting and Running a Profitable Investment Club* from the National Association of Investors Corporation, which counts 30,000 investment clubs nationwide in its membership. The book costs twenty dollars for nonmembers. You can contact NAIC at (248) 583-6242 or the Web site at www.better–investing.org.

HOW TO MANAGE SAVINGS

There are a number of factors to consider when deciding how to invest your money, including your age, current assets, and tolerance for risk. Also, no two investors have the same needs, hopes for the future, income, and existing financial responsibilities. When laying out your financial future, as well as steps to take right now, it's best to consult an accountant or financial planner, who can see the whole picture, including financial land mines that could lie ahead for you. Figure 11.2 will help you determine your savings goals.

> **DID YOU KNOW . . .**
> You can get free investment advice by attending (if you can get away) evening or Saturday morning financial seminars sponsored by brokerages in your area, some of which are probably branches of national firms. You might also, if you can, attend an adult education class in your town on a

FIGURE 11.2 WHAT ARE YOUR SAVINGS GOALS?

After you have completed it, this worksheet should help you see at a glance just where your savings are, as well as if and by how much you want to improve those balances.

SAVING/INVESTMENT	CURRENT DOLLAR BALANCE	ANY CHANGES YOU'D LIKE TO MAKE?	YOUR EVENTUAL GOAL
Life insurance			
Disability insurance			
Annuity			
Company pension			
IRA, Keogh plan			
Stocks, bonds			
Mutual funds			

topic such as "Planning for Retirement" or "Introduction to Investing." Costs for these courses are usually minimal—maybe $15 to $35.

FOR MORE INFORMATION

You can contact the American Association of Retired Persons (AARP) at (202) 434-3410 and the National Center for Women and Retirement Research at (800) 426-7386 for help in determining how much you should be saving for retirement. The American Savings Education Council offers a free worksheet, called "Ballpark Estimate," that can help you with savings planning. Contact the council at (202) 775-6364 or www.asec.org.

Part Three

HELPING YOUR LOVED ONE WITH FINANCES

$

You wonder: Does Mom have a will? Was that correction made in her pension check? How can I sell her home from 700 miles away?

You are bound to have dozens of questions like this as you set about helping your relative with health care, real estate, nursing homes, and estate planning—topics that might be totally unfamiliar to you. These next several chapters will help clear up the confusion, whether you are working with your care recipient or must make decisions on your own. Finally, Chapter 20 is a list of publications, products, and services you can get for yourself or your loved one at little or no cost.

$

CHAPTER TWELVE

A Relative's Financial Situation

As we have repeatedly mentioned, you must handle a relative's finances tactfully. If the loved one is mentally able to participate in his or her own financial decisions, then bow to those wishes, even if they are not decisions that you think are best. There are two exceptions to this rule (but even then, tread lightly): when you are concerned that a parent can't make ends meet, which is resulting in self-neglect; and when a parent is being abused financially.

MAKE CAREGIVING A GIFT, NOT A GUILT TRIP

A 1997 study by University of Florida researchers found that aging parents preferred to face the risks of caring for themselves over seeking help from their adult children. Those elderly parents whose adult children or grandchildren helped them with yard work, shopping, and transportation felt pressured to comply with their grown children's wishes, and also felt that they had to repay their children by deferring to their wishes. Elders resented this loss of power and would rather do without care—

even if they badly needed it—than pay the price of having to be deferential and obedient to their children.

However, sometimes people lack the physical or mental capacity to participate in their own financial decisions or, because of illness or disability, are unable to participate. If the problem is mental incapacity, and you have no legal right to conduct the person's affairs, then you may have to ask a court to appoint you as the loved one's guardian (more on this in Chapter 18).

Whether a loved one willingly lets you handle finances or asks for limited help, or you are appointed guardian by the court, you probably will be entering a world that is new to you, especially if you are not yet 65 yourself. You will be learning about Social Security, Medicare, Medicaid, pensions, tax benefits for the aged, and more.

DETERMINING AND LOCATING SOURCES OF INCOME

First, you must determine the care receiver's sources of income. Some checks will arrive in the mail. Other checks may not be mailed but are deposited directly into a checking or savings account. If this is the case, automatic deposits will appear on the bank statement. Every bank issues a monthly statement for accounts.

Another way to check for income sources is to review old state and federal income tax forms. Depending on the person's age, try locating at least five years' returns. The income portion of Form 1040 will show income from a former job, alerting you that a pension may be due or is already being paid. Also, sources of interest, such as savings accounts or bonds, or even rental property income, may be listed. (Keep in mind that not every state levies income taxes.)

If you need to know whether the person owns his or her own home, check with the county or city property appraisers. Check records using the property address, as the property may not be in the loved one's name.

Care receivers over age 65 or who are disabled most likely receive Social Security and perhaps disability payments or a pension. Even if the person was never employed outside the home—for example, a spouse who stayed home to care for the children while her husband worked—he or she is probably eligible for Social Security.

WHAT TO DO IF YOU CAN'T FIND FINANCIAL RECORDS

If you can't find appropriate financial records, you may have to hunt for information. Ask neighbors, friends, and other relatives. With the care receiver's Social Security number, you can ask the Social Security Administration for Form SSA-7004, Request for Earnings and Benefits Estimate Statement. The SSA will then tell you about how much the care receiver's monthly income will be when he or she is eligible to receive it.

You also can write to one or all of the major credit bureaus for a credit report. Credit bureaus are listed in the yellow pages of the telephone book under "Credit Reporting Agencies." They charge a fee for the report—usually about $10. Most reports include information such as the person's marital status, including name and age of spouse; most recent and former addresses and telephone numbers; Social Security number; bank accounts; and a credit history of the past 10 years, which includes the names and addresses of creditors.

With this information, you might learn, for example, that Aunt Mary's deceased husband, Bill, worked for the telephone company for 10 years before taking a job with the local electric company, where he worked for three years before he died. Bill may not have had a pension plan at the electric company, but he probably had a vested pension with the telephone company. Vested pensions are payable to the worker's spouse upon the worker's death, regardless of either person's age.

A government corporation, the Pension Benefits and Guaranty Corporation, can help you locate private pension plans. Its

Web site, at www.pbgc.gov, lists the names of 3,000 people with unclaimed pensions. You might learn that your father worked for the railroad and has a pension coming from that industry. The same may be true of people who served in the military.

With enough information, you can write or call these companies or the government benefits office and inquire about the benefits that are due the worker or the spouse and dependents.

Once you locate such sources and determine that benefits are due, you may have to apply for them. Each company or government agency usually has its own application form, and most will require documentation. For example, the armed forces require proof of service, using a form called DD-214. If you cannot find this form, you may have to send for a duplicate, which could take time and may require additional information.

To receive a copy of armed services records, write to the National Personnel Records Center, Military Personnel Records, 9700 Page Blvd., St. Louis, MO 63132-5100. You will need the veteran's full name, branch of service, service number or Social Security number, and exact or approximate date and years of service. If you don't have all of the information, give them what you have. Often a name and Social Security number will suffice. In a medical emergency, information from a veteran's records may be obtained by phoning the National Personnel Records Center: Army, (314) 538-4261; Air Force, (314) 538-4243; Navy, Marine Corps, or Coast Guard, (314) 538-4141.

CHECKING AND SAVINGS ACCOUNTS

If the care receiver is agreeable to making you a cosigner on his or her savings and checking accounts, so much the better. If a court has appointed you limited guardian of finances, you will have to take the court order to the financial institution to open a new account either in both of your names or in the person's name with you as the authorized signer. Requirements may vary by state. The court or an attorney can offer you direction.

SOCIAL SECURITY

As we mentioned briefly in Chapter 4, Social Security is the government program that provides retirement income to workers who, along with their employers, have paid into the fund. It also pays retirement benefits to workers' spouses, even if the spouse never worked; benefits to a spouse and minor children if the worker dies (survivor benefits); and benefits to workers if they become disabled, with additional money to their dependents. Moreover, people who have never worked or who did not earn enough credits may be able to collect benefits if they are over age 65, or are blind or disabled, regardless of their age.

In 1998, a person could begin collecting full Social Security retirement benefits at age 65 if the person was born before 1938. If you were born after 1938, the age at which you may retire with full benefits increases: If you were born in 1940, you may retire at age 65 plus six months; 1950, age 66; 1960, age 67. Individuals qualify for Social Security retirement by earning 40 credits, up to 4 a year, with one credit given for each $670 in earnings (40 credits represent 10 years of work).

Most seniors—nearly half of them—depend on Social Security as their primary source of income when they retire. According to the Social Security Administration, in 1994 the average senior's income was divided this way: Social Security, 42%; private or government pension, 18%; assets, 18%; and income from earnings, 18%.

The amount received monthly at retirement is determined by a complicated formula based on the worker's 35 highest years' earnings. Wage earners and their spouses also can elect to retire at age 62, regardless of when they were born, but that means reduced benefits. A person retiring in 1997 at age 65, who was an average wage earner, could expect to receive about $933 a month—not much to live on.

A spouse who never worked or who worked but did not earn enough credits can also collect retirement benefits beginning at age 62, although, as with the worker, benefits are reduced for retiring early. If the spouse worked, he or she can elect to take the benefit based on his or her own work record, or the other person's, whichever is higher. However, if benefits are being paid to dependents as well, there is a limit to what the government will pay.

Divorced people can elect to collect on a spouse's work record if they were married ten years and if the divorce was final two years before application is made. But if the spouse has already retired, the two-year provision is waived.

▼ DID YOU KNOW . . .
Creditors, including the Internal Revenue Service, cannot attach Social Security benefits, even with a court judgment.

SURVIVOR BENEFITS

Survivor benefits are payable to a deceased worker's family members. A widow or widower can begin collecting full benefits at age 65 (age 50 for a disabled widow[er]) or reduced benefits at age 60. However, if the widow(er) has children under age 16, or a disabled child of any age, he or she can begin receiving benefits at the worker's death. Generally these payments stop once the children reach 18 or marry. Each unmarried child under age 18 also can receive survivor benefits. And the parents of the worker, if they are age 62 or older, may also collect survivor benefits if they were dependent on the deceased worker for at least half of their support.

▼ DID YOU KNOW . . .
You can switch between benefits to whichever pays the most. If you are receiving survivor benefits, you can switch to your own retirement benefits, if they are more, as soon as you become eligible.

SUPPLEMENTAL SECURITY INCOME

If the care receiver cannot collect Social Security benefits based on his or her or on a spouse's previous wages, or if the care receiver's Social Security retirement benefits fall below certain levels, he or she may be eligible for Supplemental Security Income or the disability insurance program, if applicable.

These programs pay benefits to people age 65 or older who fall into low-income brackets, or to those under age 65 who are blind or disabled. In 1996, 6.6 million people received SSI. The average payment for one person was $254 a month for a senior, $374 for a blind person, and $385 for a person with a disability. In 1996, roughly 78% of SSI recipients were disabled, whereas 22% were seniors, mostly women. States may pay additional benefits to people meeting their own requirements.

Social Security set these guidelines as the poverty threshold for 1996 (guidelines change from time to time):

Aged person: $7,525

Family of two, headed by an aged person: $9,491

Family of four: $16,029

SSI payments may be paid to people already receiving or eligible to receive Social Security retirement income.

In addition to meeting income guidelines, people who receive SSI must also meet an assets test: Married couples must have no more than $3,000 in assets; single people are limited to $2,000. Assets, for the purposes of determining SSI eligibility, include home and land; car, up to $4,500 in value; burial plots, including those of family members; the first $1,500 of life insurance or burial funds, including those of a spouse; and the market value of personal and household goods (not the original purchase price).

Also, income limits vary by state. Most states exclude these amounts when calculating income: a small amount received each month from working or other benefits; the value of food stamps received; the value of most clothing, food, or shelter received from nonprofit organizations; and home energy assistance.

A disabled person can collect disability insurance if he or she is under age 24 and has 6 credits in a 3-year period before becoming disabled. Between the ages of 24 and 31, a person needs credits for working half the time between his or her age and the age at which he or she became disabled. A person over age 31 needs 20 credits from the 10 years immediately preceding the disability, plus 2 additional credits for each 2 years of age between 42 and 62.

If a person qualifies, his or her spouse and children may also qualify. Once approved, benefits begin six months after the date of disability and continue until the condition improves, the person returns to work, or the person reaches age 65 and converts to retirement benefits.

Despite the number of federal beneficiaries, SSI is very difficult to get, because the government's definition of disability is "a physical or mental impairment that keeps you from performing substantial work anywhere, not necessarily in your present job with your present employer." Many people hire a lawyer specializing in disability benefits to pursue their cases.

DID YOU KNOW . . .
Decisions regarding Social Security eligibility can be appealed, if you don't agree with the administration's findings. The three-step appeals process begins with a "reconsideration" and must be done within 60 days of the decision. Included in the administration's decision letter are instructions on how to file an appeal.

APPLYING FOR SOCIAL SECURITY BENEFITS

Social Security benefits can be applied for by telephone or at a local office in your community. In states where an SSI supplement is available, application may have to be made through that state office for both federal and state benefits. Bring the person's

✔ Social Security card or number

✔ Birth certificate

✔ Marriage certificate if married, widowed, or divorced

✔ Divorce papers, if applicable

✔ Children's birth certificates, when applying for survivor benefits for children under age 18, or under age 24 if they are students

⚠ CAUTION
It takes several months to begin receiving the first Social Security check, so file a few months ahead of time, if that is possible. If not, retroactive benefits can be paid for up to six months, except to those retiring early.

DIRECT DEPOSITS

The safest way to manage a care receiver's money is through direct deposit. A direct deposit occurs when the company or organization issuing the money deposits it via the Federal Deposit Insurance Corporation (FDIC) directly into a designated checking or savings account. This means checks can't get lost or stolen in the mail or at the mailbox. Often, it means the money arrives sooner, too.

Direct deposits are arranged through the company or organization issuing the check. Most check issuers require your signature on a form authorizing the direct deposit. The company or organization will need a copy of the check stub or deposit slip in order to obtain the routing information imprinted on the form.

In fact, in a money-saving move, Congress mandated that all government-issued checks be direct deposited by January 1, 1999; however, in early 1998 Congress postponed this requirement, so the effective date and requirement may change.

FILING INCOME TAX RETURNS

With a few exceptions, everyone must file an annual income tax return. Exceptions are made for those with limited income from certain sources. When would a care receiver *not* have to file? A person age 65 or older, whose filing status is single, does not have to file if his or her gross *taxable* income (which includes money, goods, property, and services) was less than $7,800. Married couples filing jointly, when both are age 65 or older, don't have to file if their combined gross *taxable* income was less than $13,800.

Every year, the Internal Revenue Service mails tax forms to taxpayers during the first week of January. The forms must be filed, unless you request an extension in writing, by that now infamous date of April 15. The form for filing an extension, Form 4868, must be filed by April 15, and it extends the filing date by two months. Be aware that an extension does not extend the deadline for when tax payments are due. If you owe taxes and do not pay them by April 15 of the year following the date of the tax return (April 15, 1998 for 1997 taxes), interest is charged for the amount owed from the time it was due. If you do not receive a tax form for the care receiver, you can pick up forms at any post office or IRS office. Forms available at post offices usually are limited to the 1040, 1040A, and 1040EZ. Additional forms are necessary if you itemize or for income other than Social Security and earnings.

If you are unsure whether the care receiver has filed a return for the most recent year or years, you can contact the IRS and have them research the account. If you do not have legal standing (power of attorney or legal guardianship for the person), you may run into problems.

If the care receiver is required to file a return but has not, you may have to file it for the person. To do that, you may have to find out more about the person's financial situation by following steps outlined at the beginning of this chapter. If all else fails, the IRS tracks taxable as well as nontaxable income assigned to individuals through forms sent by employers and other companies. For example, interest income is reported on Form 1099, along with payments of more than $600 to individuals when taxes have not already been deducted. A tax attorney, certified public accountant, or even the IRS may also be able to help. For instance, if the IRS knows of the care receiver's situation, it may waive penalties and interest while you gather information to file. The IRS routinely does this for good cause, though you may have to fill out a written request.

ELDER ABUSE AND EXPLOITATION

Most people think of elder abuse as physical harm done to an aged person. Elder abuse is much more than that. It is a growing problem that encompasses physical, mental, and financial abuse or exploitation of the elderly. That has led the federal government and states to enact stricter laws and penalties, and to step up consumer education.

The fastest-growing abuse problem is financial exploitation. From con artists to unsavory relatives to telemarketing scams, the elderly are bombarded at every level by unscrupulous people who want to separate seniors from their money.

A recent study by Princeton Survey Research, commissioned by the American Association of Retired Persons, found that Americans over age 50 are targeted by telemarketing fraud more than any other age group—56% of these victims were 50 or older, yet as a group they account for 36% of the population. This study group of elders had above average income and education and were active in their communities. The study debunks the myth that senior victims are the poorest and oldest elderly living at home alone.

Telemarketing scams, such as phony lotteries and charities, aren't the only ones around. Con artists target the elderly in person as well, in scams ranging from roof and driveway repairs to panhandling schemes—"I left my money at home, can you loan me money for a taxi because my car broke down?" Add that to thousands of mail schemes for making money at home and for free vacations.

Despite such widespread fraud, those closest to a senior can quickly wipe out the person's assets in just a matter of months. Relatives and people who befriend elders often bear watching, when certain warning signs are in place. State attorneys, social workers, and agencies that look after the elderly cite these tell-tale warning signs that an elder is being financially exploited:

- No money for bills that used to be paid on time
- Decreased amount of food in the house
- Demand letters from creditors

- Flurry of letters from banks saying accounts are overdrawn
- Electricity, water, or gas turned off
- Propensity to stay home
- Fear of a particular relative or friend

Be aware that some of these signs may also signal declining physical or mental health, so it's best to tread lightly until you know what the situation is for sure.

If you're a long-distance caregiver, you might ask that the loved one's bank notify you of large or suspicious withdrawals. If all indications point to fraud, don't try to intervene yourself, even if a family member is involved. Call the state attorney's office in the town where the elder lives and outline your suspicions. You may be required to file a formal complaint.

In many cases, the person exploiting the senior often is the senior's link to getting out of the house, eating, or to socializing. The senior may even be aware of the fraud, but does not care, so long as his or her world stays intact. When this is the case, you should take steps to ensure the elder's well-being if the suspected exploiter is removed.

Such situations may also involve mental exploitation. For instance, a caregiver may threaten the senior, "If you tell anyone that I took that money, you'll be alone the rest of your life." Fear may prevent the senior from testifying or coming clean with the facts. Always take this possibility into consideration when confronting the suspect or the elder. Sometimes, if you have proof of the exploitation but have not confronted the elder or the suspect, and the amount or item taken is inconsequential, you might want to keep it to yourself and simply find a way to remove the exploiter. Again, tread lightly here.

Physical abuse is easier to pinpoint, although harder to prove, when factors discussed above come into play. Look for cuts, bruises, burns, lumps, broken limbs, a propensity for falls, and other such signs. Again, these signs may signal a medical condition, such as vertigo or osteoporosis. A doctor's visit is in order to rule them out.

Trust is what endears con artists to seniors. Today's elders were raised in a gentler era, when a person's word meant something. Today, that is no longer true. Con men and women have perfected the illusion of trust—it's how they manage to scam so many people. Yet even legitimate salespersons can sell a senior something the person doesn't need—this might be anything from medicinal herbs and medical treatments to items that are free from a government source. For example, a person may "sell" Social Security cards. The person asks whether the elder has one; if the elder responds no, the person will say that the elder needs one. "For $20, I'll take care of this for you," the exploiter might say. Then he or she produces a standard form, obtains the necessary documentation, and may indeed send it to the Social Security Administration. Of course, this can be done over the telephone or by mail with only the cost of a phone call or stamps involved.

The best way to ward off elder abuse and exploitation is to stay in touch with elderly friends and relatives, tell them to call you if they have questions about major purchases or donations, educate them, keep telling them that "if it sounds too good to be true, it probably is," and visit them often.

You might also prepare a list of local, state, and national numbers for elderly loved ones to call to verify solicitations from insurance salespeople, charities, burial plots, and funeral expenses. You can obtain the numbers from local telephone books and consumer affairs offices.

PREVENTING ELDER ABUSE AND FRAUD

Tell seniors to:

- Be wary of door-to-door salespersons and don't invite them in.
- Ask to see identification—then call for verification—of anyone claiming to be from the IRS, Social Security, the government, a bank, or similar organizations. When you call to

verify who they are, look up the number yourself in the telephone book.

- Don't give or send money, personal identification numbers (PIN), credit card numbers, your Social Security number, or any other personal or financial information to anyone.

- Avoid sweepstakes and "free" offers.

- Hang up on telemarketers.

- Check on all contractors to make sure that they are licensed. Check the Better Business Bureau or the local consumer affairs office for a record of complaints.

- Get contracts in writing. Accept nothing orally. Don't pay for a job until it's done.

- Pay by check—never with cash.

- If they are not familiar with a charity request received over the telephone, ask for information in writing.

For information on elder abuse, call or write the National Aging Resource Center of Elder Abuse, 810 First St. NE, Suite 500, Washington, DC 20002, (202) 682-2470. The center can provide abuse hot line numbers for each state.

To report mail fraud, call or write the U.S. Postal Inspector in your area, whose number is found in local telephone books.

Report telephone fraud to the National Fraud Information Center, (800) 232-5378.

CHAPTER THIRTEEN

$

Staying at Home—and Saving

tay put? Why not?

According to surveys conducted by AARP over the years, seniors overwhelmingly prefer to remain in their own homes as they grow older. If your loved one wants to do just that, it can often be accomplished, at least for as long as possible.

Let's say it is your mother you're concerned about, in part because she lives alone. There's some work to do to enable her to stay at home, and perhaps some money to spend, too. But you'll be surprised at how many programs and services there are right in your parent's community to support you. And, since the purpose of this book is to help you with finances, you'll be delighted that some of them are free.

This chapter is for three types of readers:

- The caregiver whose recipient lives with him or her, but who could use financial and other assistance in various areas of that loved one's life.

- The caregiver whose relative lives in the same town, but not in the same residence.

- The long-distance caregiver, who might have a secondary caregiver on the scene near a relative. (There are more suggestions for caregiving from miles away, including tips for selecting a secondary caregiver, in Chapter 3.)

First, some words about your loved one's home and ideas for how he or she can save, or even earn, as much as possible from that investment.

SHARING HOUSING EXPENSES

Perhaps your loved one is still making a mortgage payment each month or writing a sizable check for rent—money that is becoming harder for the person, and maybe for you, to manage. Perhaps the mortgage is paid off, or nearly so, but your loved one could use more cash for everyday expenses.

A Roommate or Housemate

Doubling up works for young people just embarking on a career. Two roommates splitting the rent on a $600-a-month apartment can each swing $300 a lot more easily than the full rent. Add another roomie, and each sharer's rent drops to $200 a month.

Your loved one might not want *two* roommates, but one other person whose monthly rent could go toward defraying household expenses might be just what he or she needs for a bit more financial freedom.

Besides an additional income, sharing offers a senior these benefits, some of which are not so different from the reasons that younger people double up:

- Companionship
- Safety—not being alone and frightened of break-ins or of becoming ill with no one to summon help
- Help with household chores if the new sharer is fairly young

Is there a downside? There is bound to be at least some loss of privacy. Your loved one is likely to feel awkward for a while, too, having another person—perhaps a total stranger—living in his or her home. However, by making the right choice, an elderly homeowner is likely to feel comfortable in that situation fairly soon.

─────▼▼▼─────

Grief can take care of itself, but to get the full value of joy
you must have somebody to divide it with.

Mark Twain, NOTEBOOK *(1935)*

─────▲▲▲─────

You might start by helping your loved one determine the type of roommate or housemate he or she prefers. Male or female? A sharer of around the same age? Maybe your loved one would rather share with someone who is younger, who will be willing to do some home and yard work in exchange for a break on the rent. Which part of the house will that person have to him- or herself, and do those quarters need some sprucing up?

To make a match, first call your local office on aging. Many of these agencies sponsor programs to match seniors in home-sharing situations, sometimes with folks their own age, sometimes with younger people.

An office on aging is a municipal or county government agency whose phone number you should jot down because you'll probably be dialing it often. The office sponsors its own programs for seniors in the community, but it also acts as a clearinghouse, disseminating information on any topic of interest to elders and referring them to groups and associations in the particular geographic area that can be of assistance. Look under city or county listings in the government section of the phone book. It might be called "office of elder affairs" or "elder services agency" or some similar name.

You can advertise for a home sharer in the local paper, being careful to be present when your loved one interviews prospects so that you can meet them and so that all questions, on everyone's side, are answered. By all means ask for—and check—references. You and your parent should go with your instincts about a prospective sharer, too. Don't be afraid to turn down an applicant if the situation just doesn't feel "right."

It's smart to have a lease for the new roommate or housemate to sign. You can pick up a lease form at a stationery or office supply store. Fill in all blanks, even if it's just with "N/A" ("not applicable"). In some places you will probably want to write in something specific that your loved one wants or will permit. That could be "no smoking in the house" or "Jane Jones may bring her cat, Riley."

To get an idea of the amount of rent to charge, check the "Roommates Wanted" or "Apartments to Share" columns in the classified ads of your local paper.

> ▼ **DID YOU KNOW . . .**
> If your loved one lives in a city large enough to sup-
> port one, a roommate placement agency might be able to
> find a sharer. These agencies are usually geared to young
> people, but they often have a small listing of seniors. The
> fee to the agency, which might be a portion of a month's
> rent, can be paid by both parties, perhaps with the sharer
> who has the home paying less than the one looking for
> both home and roommate/housemate.

The preceding information is for the older person with a home that's too large or too costly, or both. Perhaps *your* parent would like to move into someone else's place as a sharer. A senior, too, can approach an office on aging or a roommate ser-vice. You might also put up bulletin-board notices indicating your loved one's interest in sharing. Try senior centers, social halls at houses of worship, the local AARP newsletter, and other spots likely to come to the attention of seniors.

SUBSIDIZED HOUSING FOR SENIORS

Here is a suggestion that should be raised when you are consid-ering housing options that will help your loved one to stay at home. Although this option doesn't do that, it does allow your relative to remain in his or her community. Also, it's a popular choice for many seniors.

Your loved one might move to a senior citizens rental building in your community. These can be subsidized by a religious denomination (but are generally open to all), by the state or fed-eral government, or by a combination of such sponsors. Rents, based on a tenant's income, are lower than they are for apartments on the open market. The high-rise buildings or garden complexes are often quite attractive, with lengthy waiting lists for admittance.

If you think your parent would like a particular senior complex in his or her town, call your local housing authority office for more information.

A REVERSE MORTGAGE

With a mortgage, you pay the lending institution. With a reverse mortgage, the lender pays you. That, broadly speaking, is how these relatively new (introduced in the 1980s) loan types work. They can be used with a house or a condominium, but not for a cooperative apartment or mobile home.

Your parent might want to take advantgage of this means of increasing his or her income. It's a solid concept, but it can be quite pricey, as you'll see.

It works like this. Your loved one must be at least 62 years old, have either no mortgage or just a small balance owed on the loan, and the property must be the person's principal residence. You can apply for a reverse mortgage from any number of lenders around the country and from the federal government, too. The dollar figure granted is based on the amount of equity in the person's home (usually 30% to 80% of that figure), the person's age, and the market value of that dwelling (some lenders will only consider homeowners with properties worth $75,000 or more). Lenders' terms vary. Your loved one can request a monthly income from the reverse mortgage, a lump-sum payment, or a line of credit. When the loved one moves or dies, the lender recaptures the money it advanced.

▼ **CAUTION**
There are scam artists who will offer to find your parent a reverse mortgage for a fee, usually a stiff one. There's no need to pay *anything*. Apply to lenders the way you would for any loan.

Here are some specific points you might want to consider right now.

• You and your parent should keep in mind that, naturally, a reverse mortgage and its attendant charges reduce the person's estate. Many children accept this if it allows a parent to stay in his or her home, but all of you should be aware of that fact.

• Shop around for the best terms, the way you would with any mortgage. Check with the Federal National Mortgage Association (Fannie Mae), which also offers the loans. The U.S. Department of Housing and Urban Development does, too, with its Home Equity Conversion Mortgage (HECM) program.

• Be sure you know how much a reverse mortgage is going to cost. Besides paying back the amount borrowed, the homeowner will also have to pay interest on the loan and closing costs, which can run 3% to 5% of the loan amount. That adds up! However, the federal government insures reverse mortgages to make certain that the amount a homeowner owes can never exceed the value of the home.

• Your loved one should be planning to stay in the home at least five more years. These loans are too expensive if the person will remain there just another year or so.

• Reverse mortgage payments are not taxable and do not count as income for determining eligibility for SSI or Medicaid. However, although monthly checks are not counted as income, if your loved one opts for a lump-sum payment, it could affect his or her eligibility in these areas. You should consult an elder law attorney for an explanation and guidance appropriate to your loved one's specific situation and various reverse mortgage payment programs.

• Make sure that your relative doesn't sign up for this loan at too young an age. It works best for those who are in their mid-70s or older. The younger you are, the less money you are likely to be advanced because the lender has longer to wait to get its money back.

• What happens to a reverse mortgage if your parent must go into a nursing home and leave that house or apartment? Most reverse mortgage programs address this issue, although what a homeowner must do if the situation arises can vary from one lender to another. Some lenders' plans call for repayment of the loan amount. You should be very certain your relative knows what *his or her* reverse mortgage plan calls for if a nursing home becomes a necessity one day.

Here's where you can learn more about reverse mortgages:

• *Your Retirement Nest Egg,* by Ken Scholen, has become the definitive explanation of these loans and of who lends reverse mortgage money. Scholen is founder of the National Center for Home Equity Conversion, which publishes the book. The cost is $24.95, plus $4.50 for shipping. Write NCHEC, 7373 147th St. W., Suite 115, Apple Valley, MN 55124. For credit card orders, call (800) 247-6553.

• The AARP offers free printed material on the subject. Call AARP Consumer Issues at (202) 434-2277.

• You can call Fannie Mae's public information office at (800) 732-6643.

• The HUD Housing Counselor referral line is (800) 569-4287.

SOMETHING NEW

In 1997 Fannie Mae introduced its Home Keeper for Home Purchase program. It is aimed at seniors, allowing them to buy new homes without making mortgage payments.

Imagine that your mother sells her home for $70,000, all of it equity, since the house had no mortgage. She applies to Fannie Mae for a reverse mortgage loan to buy a $120,000 house. Based on her $70,000 equity, Fannie Mae gives her a $50,000 loan at a rate that could be a point higher than a conventional mortgage. She can use Fannie Mae's $50,000, plus that $70,000, to pay for the new home, living there without making monthly mortgage payments. When she dies or moves, the loan is paid off the way it would be with a typical reverse mortgage.

Fannie Mae has more reverse mortgage programs coming up in the next few years, to allow seniors to use the dormant equity in their homes for a number of different purchases.

A BREAK ON PROPERTY TAXES

All states have property taxes. However, there are several programs in effect in many, if not most, communities nationwide to help seniors with those payments. Here are three of the most common, which are not always confined to older homeowners:

- *The Circuitbreaker,* a property tax credit whereby benefits are determined by residents' income and by property tax guidelines. There are two kinds of circuitbreakers: the sliding scale and the threshold. *Sliding-scale* programs rebate a percentage of property tax liability, whereas *threshold* programs rebate the amount of property tax that exceeds a certain percentage of a resident's income.

- *The Homestead exemption* (or *credits*), which reduces property taxes on a homeowner's primary residence by a given percentage.

- *The Deferral program,* which allows older or disabled people to put off paying property taxes until after the sale of their property or until after they have died and taxes due are paid from their estate. This is not totally free, though. Usually, a somewhat below-market interest rate is charged on the taxes that are being deferred. The tax deferral and all accumulated interest are usually represented by a lien on the homeowner's property.

Ask at the tax collector's office in your relative's town how deductions work there. Note, too, whether you must apply each year for that rate reduction. If you are not certain your parent will remember to respond to an annual notice that's mailed, you'll have to make some arrangement so that the taxation office is informed of his or her continuing interest in the reduction.

HELP WITH MORTGAGE OR RENT PAYMENTS

At hundreds of dollars each month, these expenses can seem insurmountable during a bad financial spell.

You might look to local religious groups, especially regional chapters of such nationwide nonprofit associations as, for example, Catholic Charities. When they have money available, these groups can sometimes help low-income seniors faced with eviction or foreclosure.

HOME REPAIR AND MAINTENANCE

The expense of keeping up a house can be particularly frustrating for the elderly, who can do few repairs themselves and have to worry about their cost as well. However, if your loved one is a homeowner, there may be agencies, sponsored by local government or religious-backed social services agencies, where volunteers help seniors with home repair, lawn upkeep, and snow removal. These cleanup/fix-up/paint-up programs are sometimes held once a year; sometimes they are ongoing. They are always free to the homeowner. Ask at the office on aging in your loved one's community.

HOW COMMUNITY SERVICES CAN HELP, FROM FOOD TO TRANSPORTATION

Because of the increasing number of older people in this country, many communities are boasting an ever growing number of services and programs to help their seniors, sometimes along with the disabled of any age.

Are there some programs here that could help the senior you're looking after?

FOOD

In most towns, a local government office or private social services agency sponsors a meals-on-wheels program, which delivers a hot meal at midday five days a week to elders and those with incapacitating illnesses. (In small communities there might be just one visit a week, perhaps with five frozen meals or one hot meal and frozen dinners for the other four days.)

A program bonus for older people living alone and their caregivers who live elsewhere: The individual who delivers dinner is unofficially checking on the meal's recipient and usually has a brief—very brief—moment to chat.

Sometimes there is no charge for these meals, whereas other sponsoring agencies set a fee of $2 or $3 per meal (perhaps slightly higher in some geographic areas).

Many communities have food banks, too, where those in need can "shop" for canned goods and other nonperishables. Eligibility guidelines are set by the program's sponsor.

Many elders qualify for food stamps. This is a federal program, administered by states. A monthly amount depends on the number of people in a household, income, assets, shelter cost, and other factors. In one state, for example, the range is from $10 to $218 a month.

No one should have to go hungry, and you should not have to worry about that aspect of your parent's life. Make a few phone calls, starting with the local office of elder services.

> ▼ **DID YOU KNOW . . .**
> Most hospitals and many nursing homes have dietitians on staff who can help you with specialized menus for your loved one. Home health care agencies also can frequently send a dietitian to instruct you about nutritious food preparation. Registered dietitians generally charge $60 to $80 an hour. Medicare does not cover that fee, and neither do most insurance companies.

Finally, to answer a growing need, a number of good cooks in cities and suburbs around the country have started their own home delivery service, principally to busy working households, although they'll be happy to deliver to the elderly population as well. They'll bring your loved one dinner Monday through Friday, or deliver it hot one night, along with frozen meals ready to pop into the oven or microwave, for the remaining nights. As you might expect, prices vary widely here, running about $6 to $15 a meal, including delivery.

Check the advertisements in your loved one's local newspaper for notice of this service. These small caterers might announce their business through a local eldercare office, but you can't count on it. Better look around yourself.

UTILITIES

You can ask your care recipient's utility company if his or her bills can be averaged across the year instead of having to pay especially high bills during months of greatest usage.

If your care recipient still has trouble coming up with the money and has received a final notice from a utility company, he or she can ask for assistance at the local office on aging, which often aids eligible (there are certain income criteria) seniors with utility bills.

The Salvation Army and the United Way are two other possible sources of financial aid for utility bills, as are social services agencies sponsored by mainstream religions.

You can try your loved one's telephone company to see about a limited exemption from local directory assistance charges and eligibility for a reduction in long-distance rates. Ask about any other products or services offered to seniors.

TRANSPORTATION

Your care recipient's community might be one of many around the country that has a federally funded transportation program for those with disabilities. The American Cancer Society offers cancer patients free transportation to chemotherapy treatments. A call to your relative's office on aging might put you in touch with a social services agency or a volunteer group under religious auspices that does some chauffeuring of the elderly at no cost to the passenger. That office can also tell you about public transportation discounts for seniors who travel locally.

PRESCRIPTION DRUGS

The Leukemia Society of America provides several hundred dollars per year per person for drugs used in the care, treatment, and/or control of leukemia and allied diseases. The American Cancer Society has funds for emergency situations for those who suffer from cancer.

Call your local or regional branch of an association affiliated with your relative's illness. Not all of them offer prescription assistance, but the one you need may well do so.

HOME HEALTH CARE SERVICES

The home health industry usually divides this field into two areas: (1) skilled care, which is what is provided by a registered nurse or a physical therapist, and (2) custodial care, which involves the more practical aspects of a care recipient's life, such as housecleaning and cooking, help with bathing and dressing, running errands, and providing companionship.

Nursing costs can range from $30 to $90 an hour, whereas physical and speech therapists usually charge per visit, a fee that can run from $60 up. Right now, Medicare, Medicaid, and private insurance may pay some of that cost, perhaps up to 80%.

Home health aides can provide such personal assistance as help with baths, but they cannot offer skilled nursing care. These workers may charge from $11 to $15 an hour. Medicare might cover some of that cost and so could long-term care insurance (there's more about LTC coverage in Chapter 17).

Finally, you'll find custodial care, such as homemaking and companionship, at rates of $7 to $10 an hour. These workers don't need formal training, but you should check to see if they must be registered with your state Department of Health and Rehabilitative Services. If they work for an agency registered with Medicare or Medicaid, some of their fee may be covered. Long-term care insurance might also cover costs.

You have options when deciding whom to contact: agency help or what is known as *self-hire*, which means you choose the individual you need on your own.

If you're hiring on your own, you may have to do some paperwork. For example, if the worker you hire earns more than a certain amount from you in one year, you must report those wages to Social Security and pay unemployment insurance. Your accountant can help you with the questions you are bound to have as an employer.

A home health care agency will provide you with the workers you need and will handle the necessary paperwork. That's one of the reasons for using an agency. There are now many of these agencies in existence, including some of the major national employment agencies, such as Kelly Services and Interim Personnel, which now offer health care workers, too.

Which is the better way to go? It may cost you a little less for self-hire personnel because, for one thing, you are not paying an agency's fee for finding you someone. However, the bottom line here is likely to be that you want the better worker, no matter which route he or she takes to your loved one's door.

Here are some questions to ask a potential worker you're hiring on your own or through an agency.

- What experience have you had with the elderly?
- How long can you commit to a position?
- Are there tasks that you cannot or will not perform?
- How would you handle an emergency?

Ask, too, for two work-related and at least one personal reference. And check those references!

DAY CARE/IN-HOME COMPANION OR SITTER

Adult day care can give caregivers a break from their responsibilities and the care recipient a pleasant change of scene. Day care *can* mean bringing a health aide to your home, or you might invite a volunteer, someone affiliated with a social services agency or religious group that sends companions to spend an hour or two with an ailing senior at no charge to the caregiver.

However, the term *adult day care* is more commonly used in the context of having your loved one go to a day care center one or more times a week. Activities at day care centers, which can be privately run or under local government sponsorship, include music, arts and crafts, lunch, and other leisure-time activities. Facilities vary from converted rooms in social service agency buildings to plush new quarters built for just that purpose. You can expect to pay around $50 a day for a typical center, up to $75 or so for fancy new ones. Transportation to and from the care recipient's home is sometimes included, but otherwise will cost a couple of dollars per trip. A day care center's hours are usually from 8 A.M. to 5 P.M., although a growing number offer evening and weekend hours.

You or your loved one will probably have to pick up the tab for adult day care. Some Medicaid assistance may be available, and some facilities have private and government funds to offset the cost to users of these facilities.

For the free brochure, "A Guide to Selecting an Adult Day Care Center," contact the National Adult Day Care Services Association, 409 Third St. SW, Suite 200, Washington, DC 20024, (202) 479-1200. (The number is the same as that for the National Council on the Aging. Press "O" for operator after listening to the menu.) The association is pushing for minimal requirements for adult day care facilities.

> **▼? DID YOU KNOW . . .**
> The Family Relief Program of the Alzheimer's Association pays for emergency short-term day or respite care, nursing home care, medication, medical supplies, transportation, living expenses, personal hygiene supplies, and other expenses of those with Alzheimer's disease. This "program of last resort" provides grants of up to $500 in a 90-day period. Call (800) 437-2423.

RESPITE (SHORT-TERM) CARE

For caregivers who need to get away for a few days, whether on business or vacation, or for a short hospital stay, respite care is a

FIGURE 13.1 HOW COMMUNITY SERVICES CAN HELP

Virtually every town of any size has services in place to assist the elderly and/or handicapped in a variety of areas. In the left-hand column below are some services your loved one might need (with room for you to list others). Jot down what you are paying for them now, if indeed you are able to secure them at all. Then make some phone calls to see if that aid is available locally either free or at less than your current cost.

First call your area's department of elder affairs. If it doesn't have the answers you seek, call the offices and agencies it will refer you to, both public and private. List any new charges or fees you are quoted and, finally, in the last column note your savings if you avail yourself of these newfound benefits. You will probably find that your time has been worth the effort.

NEEDED SERVICE	WHAT YOU (OR RELATIVE) PAY NOW	LOCAL AGENCY PROGRAM	COST	YOUR SAVING
Meals				
Transportation				
Help with utility bills				
Telephone checkup call				
Home maintenance				
Property tax relief				
Physical therapy or medical equipment				
Day care/ in-home companion or sitter				
Legal services				

godsend. As with adult day care, respite care can mean having a professional, or even a friend, come into your relative's home. But here, too, there is a more commonly used definition: your relative stays at a facility that accepts elders for a short visit. That means your parent can board at an assisted-living facility (ALF) or at a nursing home (there's a full explanation of both and their expenses in Chapter 14), being cared for in the same way as other residents, but for a temporary stay of anywhere from 3 to 30 days.

Rates around the country vary widely here. You might pay from $65 to $125 a day in an ALF where help is provided for bathing and dressing but there is no full-scale medical care. Nursing homes, which do provide 24-hour medical supervision, can cost from $100 to $200 a day.

Medicare, Medicaid, and long-term care insurance do not pay for respite care at an ALF or a nursing home.

Community programs can be a valuable resource. Figure 13.1 is a worksheet to help you find areas where you might be able to cut existing costs.

$

CHAPTER FOURTEEN

When It's Time to Leave Independence Behind

here may come a time when, despite your best efforts, your care recipient can no longer live alone. Perhaps your loved one realizes it, too, or, even more difficult for you, is so incapacitated that you must make all decisions now.

REVIEWING SOME CHOICES

You may want to review the suggestions made in Chapter 3, where these options were explained.

- Your parent can move in with you. You can keep your home the same as it is now, construct a bedroom-and-bath addition for the care recipient, or, if your house lends itself and local zoning laws allow, convert part of it into a full apartment for the person.

- Your parent can move to an apartment exclusively for seniors, either in his or her town or in your town, subsidized by private or government funding or both. Rents are determined by a resident's income. Living in one of these buildings or complexes will bring your parent the companionship of other residents and often provides access to a social program that might include trips to shopping facilities and errands around town. However, your parent will have no supervision and must be able to manage independently.

If those options do not seem workable, you have other housing choices.

──────▼▼▼──────

An old man loved is winter with flowers.

German Proverb

──────▲▲▲──────

ACTING ON BEHALF OF YOUR LOVED ONE

First, in considering workable choices, you will need to have your durable power of attorney or guardianship papers on hand, so that you can conduct business for your parent if he or she cannot do so. These documents will be explained in Chapter 18, although you will be familiar with most of them from reading about your own estate planning in Chapter 10. You can't conduct some of the business mentioned in this chapter without the proper authorization. Even a relatively minor point—for example, your loved one is having a rental apartment security deposit returned and you want that check sent to you—will probably mean that you must show the landlord you are legally acting for the person.

Even with these documents, you may want to consult an attorney for questions that arise while you are undertaking some of these duties.

CONTINUING CARE RETIREMENT COMMUNITY

This is one housing option your loved one might want to consider. A continuing care retirement community, usually referred to as a CCRC, is a sprawling complex that, as the name suggests, continues care from one phase of your loved one's life to the next.

A CCRC contains three lifestyle options. The first is *independent living* in a small home on the grounds. This might be a patio home, a condominium complex, a cottage, a ranch home, or even a high-rise building run under the condo form of owner-ship. There's another choice here, too: renting an apartment instead of buying. Residents in this situation are in fairly good health and lead quite independent lives, coming and going as they please. But if your parent is not able to live alone, he or she—and you—will probably find this housing style no different from the person's current living situation and therefore not a viable option.

The second phase of a CCRC might fill the bill, though. This is the *assisted-living facility,* more commonly known as an ALF (pronounced by saying its letters). Here residents receive some help with daily living—dressing, for example. Depending on the facility, your parent might have just a room and bath or an apart-ment with a small kitchen. In any event, there is always a main dining room where your parent can take meals if he or she chooses.

The third element of a CCRC is the *nursing home,* which offers 24-hour skilled nursing care. There is more about nursing homes later in this chapter.

Each CCRC is different, with its own appearance, rules and regulations, health care coverage, and, naturally, fees charged. Keep in mind, too, as you shop that many will allow you to move in only at the independent stage. Those now living in ALFs and nursing homes there had once had homes in the first living stage of that community. Be sure to check that aspect of a purchase with the complex that interests you.

DID YOU KNOW . . .

Your parent could save money by starting out in a CCRC as a tenant, to see if he or she likes life in that com-munity. Rent could be as low as $1,000 a month, which includes meals. Your parent can always buy a home there later if he or she chooses. Be sure there is a lease to sign spelling out services provided.

COSTS

You should know that continuing care *is* expensive. The flip side of that is that once you are in a CCRC, if you become ill, according to the terms of your contract, you will be cared for as long as need be. That's what has made these complexes increasingly popular over the past two decades (that and the increasing number of elderly). Indeed, most CCRCs have a policy that residents will not be forced out if they outlive their assets.

How much will this cost? First, there is an up-front fee that covers the living unit your loved one chooses and part or all of future health care costs. That can be anywhere from $10,000 to more than $500,000. Some CCRCs will return a portion of that money after a specific amount of time, if requested, or allow refunds on a sliding scale. In addition to the fee, there is a monthly cost to residents that can range from a few hundred dollars to $3,000 or more. Health care varies according to those fees and can run from total (life care) to pay-as-you-need-it services, which is what those who pay the lower entry fees often select.

▼ DID YOU KNOW . . .
CCRCs are regulated by a state's insurance department. That's because they require a substantial up-front fee that serves as a type of medical insurance. For any questions or information, contact that office in your relative's state.

Medicare and Medicaid do not normally cover assisted-living facilities. However, you should check with the department on aging in your parent's state to see if there is a statewide program that helps with ALF costs, based on financial need. Some states, such as Florida, Oregon, and Washington state, do have such coverage.

Your care recipient does not have to move to a CCRC to live in an assisted-living facility or a nursing home. There are many ALFs and nursing homes that operate independently outside CCRC borders.

GROUP HOMES AND ASSISTED-LIVING FACILITIES

These can be high-rise buildings or garden complexes with 100 or more residents, or they can be homes with as few as three bedrooms for elders. That large Victorian house at the end of your block could be an ALF home. Whatever the size of the facility, the premise is the same: offering living arrangements for seniors who do not require a nursing home but are no longer able to live alone at home either. What they provide is *custodial care,* which means room and board but no medical care. However, some may be licensed to provide simple medical services such as administering oxygen or offering counseling. These facilities must have a registered nurse or licensed practical nurse on staff.

As explained in the CCRC description of an ALF, for the most part the staff helps residents with simple daily tasks such as dressing and meals.

> **▼! CAUTION**
> The most important part of investigating any adult living community—CCRC, ALF, or nursing home—is investigating its financial soundness. Call your state office on aging for information on what you are entitled to receive from that institution (financial statements and the like). Of course, you should take all of that information to an accountant or an elder law attorney for review.

Costs vary widely for these services, according to the size and plushness of the facility, and from one part of the country to another. Remember, too, as mentioned in the CCRC description of ALFs, that the state might kick in assistance with fees for those who are eligible. If your care recipient is able to secure that aid or is paying full price in a simple facility, the lowest cost might be around $600 a month. However, the average price—a more likely guesstimate given the range of facilities nationwide—is more like $1,200 to $2,000, or even more, a month.

REGULATION

Actually, there is very little regulation of these facilities, although some states are beginning to enforce rulings pertaining to ALFs because this is such a growing field, and only more regulation-related problems are expected to surface. In some states, if an ALF serves three or fewer persons, there is virtually no regulation. Your best bet to learn about the statutes that do exist and to inquire about what to look for when shopping for one of these facilities in your area is to contact the office on aging in your parent's town or county. If this agency does not have the answers, it can steer you to state offices that will.

Finally, the checklist shown in Figure 14.1 can be used as a shopping guide for an ALF, too. Many of the points apply to both kinds of facilities.

NURSING HOMES

For caregivers, deciding to place your loved one in a nursing home is one of the most difficult decisions you can face, regardless of the fact that he or she might, for example, suffer from Alzheimer's and need 24-hour supervision. It is possible to get through this process, though, making the many decisions that are called for and knowing you have done what's best for the person you love.

MAKING THE SELECTION

What should you look for in a nursing home? The worksheet shown in Figure 14.1 will help you as you tour various facilities. It *is* important to shop around as much as you can. An on-site visit is the only way you can accurately assess what a home offers for residents—and what it lacks.

COSTS

One of the major considerations for nursing home care is, understandably, its expense. Costs are high, ranging from about

FIGURE 14.1 WHAT TO ASK ABOUT AND LOOK FOR AS YOU SHOP FOR A NURSING HOME

Make photocopies of this checklist and take one with you to each facility you visit. After you've completed your tour of nursing homes, compare them to determine the one that seems best for your relative.

Name of Facility_____

Address_____

Telephone Number_____

Name of Contact_____

(could be the person who shows you through the facility)

QUESTIONS TO ASK	RESPONSE
✔ Is a physician on staff or is primary care handled only by a resident's personal doctor?	
✔ What about the nursing staff? Is skilled nursing care available around the clock?	
✔ What about building security? Any danger of residents wandering off? If exits are locked, what would happen in the event of a fire?	
✔ Do you have recent licensing, accreditation, and inspection reports? May I see them, please?	
✔ Tell me about the cost and how that will be handled in my relative's situation.	
✔ Is there a residents' council to address problems?	
✔ Is there an advisory council for family members?	

FIGURE 14.1 (CONTINUED)

QUESTIONS TO ASK	RESPONSE
✔ Do you have a policy on residents bringing things from home, such as furniture or framed photos?	
✔ Does the facility have provisions for safeguarding personal items?	
✔ Are there activities for residents? What is the social program like?	
✔ May I tour the kitchen? Sample a meal?	

POINTS TO NOTICE	YOUR REACTION
✔ Is this location easy for family and friends to visit?	
✔ Are visiting hours convenient for you and other likely visitors?	
✔ Is the facility clean and in good repair?	
✔ Are residents clean and neatly dressed, appearing cared for?	
✔ Are there any odors, aside from cooking smells at mealtimes?	
✔ Are there safety systems, such as grab bars along hallways and in rooms, especially bathrooms?	
✔ Watch signal lights that residents press to call for assistance. How long does it take for help to arrive?	
✔ Are residents who cannot feed themselves being helped?	

FIGURE 14.1 (CONTINUED)

POINTS TO NOTICE	YOUR REACTION
✔ Look at residents in restraints. Are there many of them? (If yes, that's not a good sign.)	
✔ Talk to some residents and staff members. Do they seem reasonably happy with the facility and with their jobs?	

Note: Try to drop in unannounced and at a busy time of day, during morning wake-up or at mealtime. The atmosphere may be totally different from what you experienced at a time when guests were expected.

$80 to more than $150 a day in some facilities, and that may not include some services, such as personal laundry and medication.

As mentioned earlier in this chapter, your loved ones are pretty much on their own in paying for nursing home care. Payment comes either from the person's savings or from long-term care insurance. (Medicare pays for only short-term nursing home care, following an elder's hospitalization. See Chapter 16, on Medicare and Medicaid, which discusses nursing home expenses.)

Here are two suggestions, if your loved one does not want to deplete savings, which he or she probably sees as a diminishing inheritance for children and perhaps others he or she would like to remember. Seeing their hard-earned money disappear into nursing home costs is a great fear among elderly people.

- *A reverse mortgage.* Now that it is not possible for your relative to remain at home, he or she might use this income source for nursing home bills.

- *A viatical settlement on the person's life insurance policy.* This involves paying about 80% of the value of the policy to the policyholder immediately. It is an option for those who have a doctor-certified life span of two years or less. This will be explained further in Chapter 17.

If your parent is not able to manage either of these opportunities alone, see if your power of attorney or guardianship allows you to act on his or her behalf. With all of the paperwork to plow through in a nursing home admission, you will almost certainly want to seek legal counsel—if possible, from an elder law attorney.

Figure 14.2 lists the legal rights of a nursing home resident.

Besides checking out nursing homes to find the best place for your loved one, you can contact the office on aging in his or her community for printed material on nursing homes. Ask, too, for information about state licensing, accreditation, and inspection reports of these institutions.

The National Association of State Units on Aging, at (202) 898-2578, can give you the name of the ombudsman in your loved one's state to contact for nursing home information. If you are utilizing the services of a geriatric care manager, he or she

FIGURE 14.2 RIGHTS OF NURSING HOME RESIDENTS

Federal laws, as well as some state laws, spell out rights for nursing home residents. The basics of Federal Statutes, Public Law 10203, Subtitle C., Section 4201, follow.

Residents have the right

- to examine a facility's latest state inspection report and have a copy of its rules, with explanations as requested
- to inspect and get copies of all personal records
- to be fully informed of medical care
- to participate in planning personal care
- to refuse medical treatment
- to manage one's own financial affairs
- to be informed in writing of Medicaid, Medicare and other insurance reimbursements, as well as charges those payers don't cover
- to choose a personal attending physician and to contact another physician, such as one on a nursing home's staff
- to privacy, including written communications
- to have regular access to a private phone
- to keep and use personal clothing
- to be transferred or discharged only for medical reasons (30-day written notice); other residents' welfare (30-day written notice); or nonpayment (15-day written notice).

can offer an honest assessment, based on personal experience, of some specific nursing homes you may be considering. If you do not have such a manager, you could engage one for an hour or so to ask about nursing homes in your area.

Several sources offer printed material on this subject:

- The American Association of Homes and Services for the Aging, 901 E St. NW, Washington, DC 20004, (202) 783-2242.

- For the free brochure, "Nursing Home Life: A Guide for Residents and Families," contact the AARP at 601 E St. NW, Washington, DC 20049, or (800) 424-3410.

- For a copy of the book, *Nursing Homes: Getting Good Care There,* by the National Citizens' Coalition for Nursing Home Reform (NCCNHR), send a check for $17 (includes shipping) to NCCNHR, 1424 16th Street NW, #202, Washington, DC 20036, or call (202) 332-2275. This group offers free printed material as well.

CAUTION

Are you automatically thinking of bringing your relative home to your community, to a nursing home there? Your loved one may have numerous friends, and perhaps even some family members, where he or she is living now, so that the loved one might have more visitors in a facility there than you and your family, however well meaning, will be able to manage if you move the person to your area. And visitors, of course, notice the care a resident receives, which is beneficial.

IF YOUR LOVED ONE NOW RENTS AN APARTMENT

Chapter 3 discussed breaking a lease. It was directed at caregivers who move to where the loved one lives. However, this section discusses the possibility of the care *recipient* giving up an apartment or house he or she currently rents.

Your care recipient might have an easier time getting out of a lease than you would, depending on landlord/tenant laws where you live. In some states there is a provision for terminating a lease in certain situations. In New York, for example, a senior has the right to cancel a rental agreement if he or she is entering a skilled nursing facility. Check your parent's local housing office for regulations there.

Even if there is no legal provision for exiting a lease, many landlords will be reasonable if it is a senior who is involved, because that usually means a move to a place where care is needed, whether that place is an adult child's home or a nursing home or similar facility.

Regardless of whether your relative has a lease, try to give the usually required 30-day notice of leaving, if that is possible. That can be especially important if your loved one has lived on those premises for a number of years. The landlord will no doubt have a good deal of painting and some repairs to do in that apartment and will appreciate having time to line up work crews so that the unit is not vacant, with no rental money coming in, for too long a time. The benefit to you in giving notice might be an easier time getting out of the lease and the return of the security deposit.

Make an effort to leave the premises in good condition, too, so that the deposit will be returned—although, quite honestly, that may not be possible if your relative leaves before the term of the lease has expired. Leave your own or your parent's address with the landlord anyway, in anticipation of the check for the security deposit. It should be in the mail within two to four weeks (depending on local law) of leaving the place in satisfactory condition.

PREPARING A HOME FOR RENT OR SALE

If your parent is entering a nursing home with no expectation of one day being able to leave that facility, you may be faced with the decision of what to do about the person's now-empty house or condominium. The decisions you will be able to make in this area will depend in great measure on the power of attorney or guardianship you hold. For example, some states allow the sale of an incapacitated homeowner's property by power of attorney, while others do not.

Also, keep in mind that you do not have to sell your parent's home for him or her to qualify for Medicaid, if that concerns you. Owning a home is allowed under Medicaid requirements. Also, by selling, you are creating cash assets for the person that would be exempt from Medicaid consideration if they were to remain as real estate. Talk to your attorney.

You could rent out the house, bringing your parent some perhaps much-needed income. You can ask a local management company how much it would charge to rent and manage the property for you if you live some distance away.

For family and economic reasons, you might want to sell the house, if you have the legal authority to do so. By all means discuss this with family members. You may have siblings who, along with you, stand to inherit that property. It's a good idea to discuss this family-related aspect of the sale with an attorney.

With everything else you have on your mind these days, it is not likely you will want to handle the sale yourself. Call three real estate agents and ask them to look at your parent's home to give you a no-cost *comparative market analysis* (CMA) of the dwelling. A CMA is a listing of what homes in the immediate area have sold for in the last year or so and the number of days they were on the market. Each agent will also give you a recommended asking price and a probable selling price for the home.

▼ **DID YOU KNOW . . .**

You do *not* have to sign up with any realty agent who offers you a comparative market analysis. This is a free service that almost all realty people offer home sellers in the hope that they will get their listings.

Keep in mind that the agent who gives you the highest likely sale price is not necessarily the one who will do the best job for you. The agent could be proposing that figure just to get your listing. Be realistic about the pluses and minuses of your parent's home.

A house for sale always sells faster and at a better price if it looks airy and roomy (and clean, naturally). You may—or probably will—want to wait until your parent has moved before placing the house on the market. Many elders' homes are filled with collections, photographs, and other furnishings accumulated over the years. Although, traditionally, a furnished home shows better than an empty one, in your case an empty, freshly painted (if possible) home might look better than a cluttered one.

> **? DID YOU KNOW . . .**
> Up to 1997 there was a federal tax break known as the "over 55" exemption. Home sellers 55 years of age or older were entitled to deduct, one time only, the first $125,000 of profit on that home if they were married, and the first $62,500 if single. Now for all sellers regardless of age the first $250,000 ($500,000 for a married couple) of profit from their home sale is exempt from capital gains tax. It's not a one-time deal either, although sellers must have lived in that home for at least two years.

SELLING A HOME AS A LONG-DISTANCE CAREGIVER

It could be easier than you think to sell your parent's home if you live a few hundred or a few thousand miles away. Here is why.

You can visit a local franchise of a nationwide real estate company, which can work with a colleague from that firm in your parent's town or region. The sale can be handled through phone calls and fax messages between the two offices. Don't forget to ask the agent in your parent's community to send you the comparative market analysis.

While it is not smart to have a proxy represent you when you are *buying* a home (there are many details that buyers will want to handle for themselves), as a *seller* you can, if you choose, designate the real estate agent in your parent's town to be at the closing in your place. There are fewer items that require the signature of the seller, and, overall, the closing process is simpler for that party.

DID YOU KNOW . . .
You can have a *limited* or *special power of attorney* for a one-time transaction, such as a house closing that might be taking place out of town.

Since you are likely to be in your parent's town to help with the move, you can introduce yourself to the real estate agent at that time, before returning to your home.

CLEARING OUT AND CLEANING UP

One particularly time-consuming aspect of selling your loved one's home is what to do with furniture and everything else that composes that household.

There are tips for getting rid of household stuff in Chapter 3, where you read about cleaning out your own home if you are moving to be closer to your care recipient. These include the ubiquitous garage sale, a tag sale, giving certain items to charity, and so on. Refer to Chapter 3 for some ideas on downsizing your parent's furnishings.

There are some important points in this situation that did not apply in the chapter about your own move:

- It will help if you know before the move just where your parent is going so you can anticipate needs based on the space available in the new accommodation. You can then mentally furnish it and you will know what will have to be given away or sold.

- If your parent can participate in discussions, by all means he or she should have a say about what goes and what stays. A 10-piece dining room set is not likely to fit into an assisted-care facility, no matter how much your parent wants to keep it, but other than impractical wishes, let him or her decide.

- Be careful not to sell or give away items that might be mentioned in your parent's will as a bequest to a beneficiary. If your parent is unable to identify these items, and if you do not have access to the will, you will just have to use common sense. Talk to members of the immediate family to reach some agreement on these types of decisions.

CHAPTER FIFTEEN

$

Getting the Most from Health Insurance

▼▼▼

When the praying does no good, insurance does help.
Bertolt Brecht, THE MOTHER *(1932)*

▲▲▲

Whether your loved one is age 55, 65, or 90, there is a health insurance plan to help pay for a doctor, hospital bills, and other medical services. Unfortunately, few health care plans pay for the care that is most needed later in life: long-term care. Still, the longevity of this generation has not gone unnoticed, and a variety of long-term care plans are becoming available. They are expensive, and the older the insured person is, the more cost-prohibitive such policies become. Long-term care insurance is not really considered health insurance (because it covers expenses that are not *medically necessary,* a phrase you'll be hearing more of); long-term care insurance is explained in Chapter 17.

This chapter focuses on health insurance: traditional fee-for-service policies, health maintenance organizations, CHAMPUS (Tricare), and veterans affairs benefits, as well as insurance policies that fill in the gap—CHAMPUS supplements. Disease-specific policies also are discussed in Chapter 17.

TRADITIONAL INSURANCE

Seniors may have traditional fee-for-service insurance if they still work or as part of a company retirement plan. Some companies offer lifetime health care insurance to their employees as part of a retirement package, but benefits can change over the years. Other seniors may be under 65 and still carry a traditional insurer.

Regardless of the circumstances, such plans are governed by the senior's or the employer's contract with the insurance provider.

If a senior is fortunate enough to have both Medicare and a health plan, Medicare becomes the secondary payer. This means it covers costs the primary plan does not pay for (such as a 20% copayment), as long as the charge is one that Medicare would cover.

Traditional insurance may be provided by an employer through a group plan, or individuals can purchase a policy—although the cost is usually steep.

HOSPITAL/SURGICAL PLANS

An individual also can purchase a hospital/surgical plan, which covers hospital and doctor charges with a small deductible, or a comprehensive/major medical policy, which has higher limits and deductibles. For most seniors, such plans usually are unaffordable.

If a senior still works, the Health Insurance Portability and Accountability Act of 1996 guarantees that workers can continue their health insurance coverage, regardless of preexisting conditions, if they lose or change jobs.

MEDICAL SAVINGS ACCOUNTS (MSAs)

While not really health insurance per se, medical savings accounts were established by Congress as another part of the Health Insurance Portability and Accountability Act of 1996.

An individual can deposit up to $2,000 a year in pretax dollars ($4,000 for a family) into a savings account with use restricted to paying everyday health care expenses. The account must be accompanied by a low-cost, high-deductible catastrophic medical insurance policy, which would cover major medical expenses.

The interesting part is that pretax money is used to fund the account, and account earnings are tax deferred. At the end of each year, money remaining in the account can be rolled over into the next year or withdrawn and used, but not without a tax penalty. So a medical savings account is similar to an IRA.

Congress authorized MSAs as a four-year pilot program that began January 1, 1997. MSAs are limited to 750,000 people on a first come, first served basis. Only people who are self-employed or uninsured or who work for a company with 50 or fewer employees are eligible to participate.

The cost of major medical insurance averages $1,500 for a single person to $3,000 for a family. Most policies have a lifetime maximum benefit, usually around $2 million. Major medical usually carries an annual deductible, but doesn't require copayments.

Some of the benefits of an MSA are:

- It is an incentive for Americans to save and stay healthy, because unused money stays in an individual's savings account.

- It encourages control of a person's own health care dollars.

- It allows a choice of doctors, hospitals, and other health care providers.

Others argue that the poor cannot afford the plan and, to save money, will not seek medical care. As a result, people with ongoing medical problems will pay more for health care.

MSAs are definitely a better deal when you're young, but a healthy older person might benefit, too.

Assuming an 8% return, a 20-year-old who invests $1,800 a year in an MSA would have $11,404 in the account at the end of 5 years, $142,118 after 25 years, and $751,367 after 45 years at age 65. This assumes the person has no medical expenses, but you can see how the money adds up. Assuming this same person paid $1,000 a year for medical expenses over the 45 years, he or she would still have $333,941 upon retirement.

This money could be used to fund long-term care expenses, such as nursing or home health care, or the unused money could be left to heirs.

MEDICAL CLAIMS SERVICES

Tracking medical bills and payments can quickly turn into a nightmare when a loved one has a serious or ongoing illness.

Medicare mails statements and cost-share bills; doctors, hospitals, and labs send more. Some include payments already made or show that Medicare or another insurer was billed; others don't. It's no wonder caregivers increasingly turn to medical claim companies to sort out the mess.

Did the hospital file claims with Medicare and Medigap? Did the insurer refuse to pay for a procedure when the policy says it's covered?

For a fee, medical claim companies can take this worry off your shoulders. They look for billing errors that may save you money, file claims, follow up on payments, and more.

These companies charge per project, at a cost of $30 to $80 an hour, or an annual fee that can run from $15 to $200 a year for unlimited assistance.

To find a claims service near you, contact the National Association of Claims Assistance Professionals, which provides referrals to a member in your area. Call or write (708) 963-3500, 4724 Florence Ave., Downers Grove, IL 60615. You also can check the yellow pages of your telephone book for listings under "Insurance Claim Processing Services."

> **?** **DID YOU KNOW . . .**
> United Seniors Health Cooperative members—and their friends—can subscribe to the nonprofit organization's Medical Bill Minder, a health insurance claims service for $15 per person. Call (800) 659-3171 for more information.

If money is a concern, Medicare offices and local offices on aging may be able to provide free help or refer you to a group or organization that can help.

Nearly every state also has a SHINE program (Serving the Health Insurance Needs of Elders). Senior volunteers are trained to help other seniors and their caregivers on insurance matters.

MANAGED CARE

Managed care is *the* insurance of the 1990s and most likely will be the insurance of the new millennium. Such plans are known as *health maintenance organizations* (HMOs) or *preferred provider organizations* (PPOs), with some hybrids in between.

HMOs have gained in popularity primarily because the cost of health care—and health care insurance—has risen so dramatically. HMOs offer lower premiums, because of the way care is provided.

With traditional insurance, you choose any doctor (including specialists when they are needed), hospital, or other health care providers and pay a copayment, traditionally 20% of the charge.

Under an HMO, you use the HMO's network of primary care physicians, who serve as gatekeepers of your care. The primary care physician tells you when you need a specialist, and when you do, you must go to your HMO's network of specialists.

Obviously, you are trading choice for cost, but for some people this isn't a problem—for example, when you haven't found a doctor you like, your doctor has retired, or you're new to an area. It's also possible that your favorite doctor already is a member of the HMO's network. Ask your doctor which HMOs he or she is affiliated with, or ask the HMO for a list of doctors.

> **▼ CAUTION**
> Your HMO doctor today may not be your doctor tomorrow. HMOs drop doctors and doctors drop HMOs.

The same holds true for specialists, hospitals, and other health care providers. If you have a preferred hospital or cardiologist, for example, check with them or the HMO to see if they are in the plan you're considering.

Unlike most traditional insurance, HMOs stress preventative care and often pay for services not covered by traditional insurance, such as eye exams and glasses, hearing tests and hearing aids, dentists and dentures.

Seniors who travel frequently or for long periods of time may want to think twice about an HMO because, except for emergencies, an HMO will not pay for doctors and hospitals not in its network. If your parent stays with you half a year and with another relative half a year, an HMO may not be a good idea.

Before you join an HMO, compare companies. Find out what services are covered and ask for a list of providers. Also, ask about coverage for preexisting medical conditions.

HMOs can be group plans, individual policies, or Medicare and Medicaid policies. In 1995, about one fourth of all Medicaid recipients—11.6 million people—were enrolled in managed care plans. On January 1, 1997, 13% of Medicare beneficiaries, or more than 4.9 million people, were enrolled in 336 managed care plans. Some considered an HMO an alternative to Medigap. (You'll read more about Medigap in the next chapter.)

Like other people enrolled in HMOs, Medicare beneficiaries can enroll or disenroll in a managed care plan at any time and for any reason with only 30 days' notice. With this in mind, you might consider trying an HMO to see if you like it.

In addition to the regular services covered under Medicare, managed care plans often cover preventative care, prescription drugs, eyeglasses, dental care, and hearing aids.

How much you can save with an HMO over traditional insurance will depend on a number of factors, including your age and where you live.

HMOs, as large companies, negotiate discounted prices with health care providers, including hospitals, doctors, and therapists. All of the providers they contract with are paid a set amount, called a *capitation rate,* to care for you. If you don't get sick, the provider makes money. If you get sick, the provider loses money. There also may be incentives for providers who help keep costs down, and this is one of the biggest complaints heard about HMOs.

The HMO tells doctors when they are allowed to give you blood tests, X rays, and other medical tests, and under what conditions you can be referred to a specialist. By keeping a tight rein on the purse strings, the HMO makes money. Consumers have complained loudly about this aspect as well, and HMOs have listened.

Despite the drawbacks, HMOs are probably here to stay. Governments began exploring HMOs to bring down the costs of both Medicare and Medicaid. So today HMOs are available for both of these federal programs, and the number of people joining these organizations is growing rapidly. Congress has and will continue to explore ways to encourage seniors to join Medicare HMOs.

In the end, only you can decide if an HMO is best for you or a loved one.

DID YOU KNOW . . .
If you want to explore the downside of HMOs, visit the Physicians Who Care Web site at www.hmopage.org.

INSURANCE RATING COMPANIES

Once you've narrowed down your choice of HMOs (or any other insurers), check the company's financial records. In the 1980s and 1990s, some large insurance companies failed, leaving thousands of people without coverage.

With this in mind, you should research the financial stability of any insurance company you are considering. Start by getting a copy of its most recent financial statement. Ask the company for one, or call your state department of insurance. Another place to check is with a company that independently reviews and rates the financial soundness of insurers. Check the library for listings, or call the company directly. If you call, you will be charged for the service, either by the minute or per request.

There are several rating companies, and each uses a different scoring system. For example, Standard & Poor's and Duff &

Phelps call their best rating "AAA," while Moody's Investors Services' highest rating is Aaa, and A.M. Best's is A++. Obviously, you will want to purchase insurance from companies that are the most fiscally sound, and hence have a high rating.

HELP IN DECIDING ON INSURANCE

If you can't decide which way to go or you are unsure of which type of insurance is best for you or your loved one, check with the agency on aging in your community for the name and telephone numbers of volunteer groups (such as SHINE, discussed above) that can help you decide. Volunteers won't make the choice for you, but they will look at your individual circumstances and resources and make recommendations.

CHAMPUS/TRICARE

CHAMPUS (Civilian Health and Medical Program of the Uniformed Services) is the government's health insurance plan for active-duty military personnel and their families, military retirees and their families, and certain government workers. In recent years, the name of this program has been changed to Tricare, with three levels of service now available. Tricare is a managed care program.

Many armed forces retirees who have put in 20 years of service are not yet 65, so they continue to be covered under CHAMPUS until they are eligible for Medicare. With some exceptions, all retirees must change coverage from CHAMPUS to Medicare when and if they are eligible.

Military retirees who do not choose the higher levels of Tricare, called Tricare Extra and Tricare Prime (for which they pay an annual fee and are guaranteed access to military physicians, specialists, and facilities) remain under the old CHAMPUS coverage, now called Tricare Standard. This coverage pays 75% of medically necessary care and services similar to those covered by

Medicare, such as doctor bills, hospital bills, diagnostic tests and treatment, medical supplies, rehabilitation care, durable medical equipment, some organ transplants, skilled nursing care, and hospice care. Retirees pay the other 25%, plus an annual deductible. After a retiree has paid $7,500 during the fiscal year (October 1 through September 30) in out-of-pocket medical expenses, CHAMPUS pays 100% of the remaining bills, thus acting like a catastrophic insurance policy.

CHAMPUS does not cover custodial care, but may cover some limited skilled nursing services, prescription medicines, and up to 12 physician visits a year, even if a condition is considered custodial.

▼ DID YOU KNOW . . .
Retirees of any age may continue to receive prescription medications free from military facilities.

VETERANS ADMINISTRATION BENEFITS

In 1942, the peak of World War II, 12 million men and women served in the armed forces. That puts their ages at about 74 now. And, because they served their country, they may be eligible for veterans benefits that pay for medical care, hospitals, home health care, and nursing home care.

Eligibility is determined by two categories. Category 1 includes those disabled while serving their country and veterans who were not disabled, but whose income and net worth fall below certain levels. Category 2 includes all others.

Category 1 veterans are eligible to receive free hospital and outpatient care. Category 2 veterans may use VA facilities and services on a space-available basis, but they pay a copayment for services and facilities: $10 a day for hospital care and $5 a day for VA nursing home care. For outpatient care, the copayment is 20% of the cost of an average outpatient visit. Category 2 veterans eligible for Medicare are responsible for paying the Medicare deductible for the first 90 days of hospital care in any

365-day period. For each additional 90 days of hospital care, they pay one half of the Medicare deductible.

The VA also pays for some nursing home care, using the same criteria for hospital care. Category 1 veterans also receive first priority for nursing home admissions. Full coverage of nursing care is limited to:

- Veterans requiring nursing care for a service-connected disability after medical determination by the VA
- Patients in a military hospital requiring a protracted period of nursing care and who will become veterans upon discharge from the armed forces
- Veterans discharged from a VA medical center
- Veterans receiving home health services from the VA

All other veterans must make a copayment. With few exceptions, the VA seldom pays for more than six months of nursing home care.

APPLYING FOR VA BENEFITS

To apply for VA benefits, a veteran needs a number of documents, including Social Security card or number, birth certificate, marriage license(s), insurance policies, statement of Social Security benefits, and military service records.

In determining need under Category 1, the VA calculates the income of both spouses. Social Security, pensions, wages, interest, and other government compensation are included. Assets countable for the means test include stocks, bonds, IRAs, and savings, but not the primary residence and personal property.

VA RESOURCES

The VA has a number of resources. For questions, call (800) 827-1000. For interactive help or to read or download publications, visit the VA Web site at www.va.gov. In addition, you can pick up a copy of the booklet, "Federal Benefits for Veterans and Dependents," at any VA center.

DID YOU KNOW . . .
Paralyzed Veterans of America is a Washington, D.C.–based advocacy group for veterans, providing free referrals, literature, and other help. Call (202) 872-1300.

CHAMPVA

CHAMPVA, the Veterans Administration Civilian Health and Medical Program, shares the cost of medical care for dependents and survivors of veterans. If a veteran is not eligible for CHAMPUS or Medicare Part A, he or she might be eligible for CHAMPVA. People who qualify are:

1. The spouse or child of a veteran who has a permanent and total service-connected disability

2. The spouse or child of a veteran who died of a service-connected condition, or who, at the time of death, was permanently and totally disabled from a service-connected condition

3. The spouse or child of a person who died in the line of duty, not due to misconduct, within 30 days of entry into active service

Beneficiaries age 65 or older who lose eligibility for CHAMPVA by becoming potentially eligible for Medicare Part A or who qualify for Medicare Part A benefits on the basis of a disability may reestablish CHAMPVA eligibility by submitting documents from the Social Security Administration certifying they are not entitled to or have exhausted Medicare Part A benefits.

On the other hand, people under age 65 who are enrolled in both Medicare Parts A and B could become eligible for CHAMPVA as a secondary payer to Medicare.

To see if your loved one qualifies or to apply for benefits, write or call CHAMPVA Center, P.O. Box 65024, Denver, CO 80206-5024, (800) 733-8387.

CHAPTER SIXTEEN

$

The Two Big *M*s:
Medicare and Medicaid

MEDICARE

Medicare is the primary source of health insurance for the elderly and the disabled. In 1996, over 95% of the country's aged and disabled, about 38 million people, were enrolled in Medicare. And Medicare paid over $200 billion in medical expenses for them, averaging $5,302 per person.

To refresh your memory, Medicare is a two-part program: Part A covers hospital charges, home health care, and similar charges; Part B covers doctor bills, plus a host of miscellaneous items outlined later in this chapter.

When a person turns age 65 and applies for Social Security retirement benefits, he or she is automatically enrolled in Medicare Part A; there is no premium. Part B carries a monthly premium—$43.80 in 1998—which is automatically deducted from the recipient's Social Security check or is billed each month if the recipient does not receive Social Security income. Part B is not mandatory but becomes available when a person turns 65. If a person decides not to enroll at 65, he or she loses the opportunity to enroll for another year. The annual enrollment period is from January 1 to March 31.

If a person is permanently and totally disabled but not yet 65, he or she can receive Medicare, if the person has received Social Security benefits for 24 months.

▼! CAUTION
Medicare imposes a penalty on people who are eligible to enroll in Part B but who decline: Premiums are increased 10% for each year the person was eligible to enroll but did not. Exception: People covered by an employee health plan.

People who don't qualify for Social Security can buy in to Medicare at a cost of $309 (in 1998) a month for those 65 or older, or $187 (in 1998) a month for those who already have 30 credits toward Social Security. As you may recall, with some exceptions, you must have 40 credits earned by working over a period of years to be eligible for Social Security.

The best thing about Medicare is that, once minimum requirements are met, an eligible person cannot be refused coverage for preexisting conditions.

Medicare is paid for by workers through payroll taxes that are matched by their employers, the same as with Social Security. Although the government collects the money, the insurance plan is administered by 32 insurance carriers, such as Blue Cross and Blue Shield companies.

You can receive a free handbook on Medicare coverage by calling the Social Security Administration, (800) 772-1213, or the Medicare hot line, (800) 638-6833.

▼? DID YOU KNOW . . .
If a low-income person cannot afford Medicare Part B monthly premiums or copayments and deductibles, he or she may be eligible to receive them free through the Qualified Medicare Beneficiary Program. To qualify, income can be up to 120% of the poverty level. Apply through your state's Medicaid program (but you don't have to be on Medicaid).

MEDICARE COVERAGE

Of course, Medicare doesn't cover everything, nor does it pay 100% of medical bills. Part A covers a semiprivate hospital room and meals, special care units, diagnostic tests such as X rays, laboratory work, operating and recovery room, intensive care, anesthesia, rehabilitative services, skilled nursing, home health care and hospice care, and medically necessary services and supplies provided in the hospital.

When ordered by a doctor as medically necessary, Medicare will pay for up to 28 hours per week of skilled nursing and home health aide services. The number of hours for which Medicare will pay for home health care is decreasing. It could pay for service indefinitely with no copayment if the plan administrator approves. However, the person needing care must:

- Require and receive intermittent skilled nursing, or physical, occupational, or speech therapy.
- Be homebound (cannot leave home without assistance).
- Have the service ordered under a physician's plan of care.
- Be provided services through a Medicare-approved agency.

Care in a skilled nursing facility, such as a nursing home, is covered under Part A, if it follows within 30 days of a hospital stay of at least 3 days and is *medically necessary*. In a nursing facility, services covered are similar to those of a hospital stay, but also include coverage for rehabilitation services and appliances.

As mentioned, in order for Medicare to pay for these services, they must be *medically necessary*. That means a doctor says they are needed. For example, in order for Medicare to pay for a nurse to come to your home, the care must be related to the illness for which the person was in the hospital, and the nursing services must be for medical care related to that illness, such as intravenous therapy. If a senior is weak after being discharged from the hospital and needs help getting from the bed to the bathroom or needs help preparing meals or even eating, Medicare will not pay for nursing services because these services are not *medically necessary*.

These two words are key to paid coverage. Too many people think that Medicare will cover long-term care in a nursing home, but it will not. Medicare pays for short-term care.

▼ DID YOU KNOW . . .
In 1998, Medicare began covering mammography, pap smears, and colorectal cancer screenings. These screenings are exempt from deductibles and copayments.

COPAYMENTS AND DEDUCTIBLES

For hospital charges, your loved one pays a deductible of $764 (in 1998) for each benefit period. A benefit period starts when the person is admitted to the hospital and ends 60 days after discharge. After 60 days, the patient pays $191 a day (in 1998).

Medicare pays only for charges it approves, and at a specific rate.

If a loved one needs more than 90 hospital days, the person can draw from a bank of 60 days, a lifetime reserve, for which the copayment is $382 (in 1998) a day. Medicare will not pay anything after 150 days.

▼ CAUTION
The lifetime reserve is very important should a person become critically ill. Don't let a long-term acute care hospital needlessly use up these benefits.

Similarly, the loved one pays nothing for 20 days of skilled nursing (nursing home care) if he or she is receiving therapy and progressing. However, the resident pays $95.50 (in 1998) a day for the 21st to 100th days. Medicare pays nothing after 100 days.

▼ DID YOU KNOW . . .
Nursing homes can no longer request deposits from Medicare beneficiaries to cover days 21 to 100.

Medicare Part B pays for doctors and surgeons, clinical laboratory tests, outpatient services, physician assistants, some psychiatric care, chiropractors, ambulance, durable medical equipment, medical supplies, prosthetics, mammograms, injectable drugs for osteoporosis and physical and speech therapy, flu vaccinations, and prescription drugs.

The deductible is $100 per year and the care receiver makes a 20% copayment.

▼ CAUTION

Medicare does not limit outpatient charges, so hospitals and outpatient clinics can charge as much as the market will bear. This means your loved one pays not only 20% of the amount Medicare approves, but any amount over that. Ask about charges for outpatient services and what Medicare pays for that same service.

Example: Clinic charges $100; Medicare approves $80. You pay 20% of $80 ($16) *plus* another $20.

Now that you know what Medicare will pay for, here is a list of services it will *not* cover:

- Private hospital room
- Long-term nursing home care
- Personal or custodial care
- Long-term nursing
- Homemaker services (except for hospice)
- Home-delivered meals
- Routine eye exams
- Contact lenses (except lenses for some cataract surgery)
- Dentures and dental care

Doctors are not required to participate in Medicare; they elect to do so. Once a year, a doctor may elect to take Medicare assignment, which means he or she will accept as full payment the amount Medicare pays. If the doctor does not file for this election, he or she may still accept Medicare, but cannot charge you more than 15% of Medicare's set charge (some states limit this percentage even further). Doctors also are required to fill out the Medicare forms required for payment and mail them for you.

You can obtain a directory of doctors in your area who accept Medicare assignment by calling (800) 333-7586, or ask your doctor if he or she accepts Medicare assignment.

▼**DID YOU KNOW . . .**
You can appeal any Medicare decision, but you must do so within 60 days of being notified of the decision.

MEDIGAP

As you can see, Medicare doesn't pay for everything. With a serious illness or surgery, deductibles and copayments will add up quickly. To provide relief from such costs, private insurers offer a policy that fills in the gaps, aptly called Medigap.

Federal law limits insurance companies to 10 uniform Medigap plans. The law also requires that everyone eligible for Medicare be guaranteed Medigap coverage, if they choose, within six months of turning age 65. A person cannot be denied Medigap for preexisting conditions and can cancel a Medigap policy within 30 days of its delivery.

▼**DID YOU KNOW . . .**
Department of insurance and Social Security offices in most states offer Medigap counseling programs, or call the national Medigap hot line, (800) 638-6833.

MEDIGAP PLANS

The 10 plans are identified by the letters A through J. None can offer benefits already covered by Medicare. Plan A is the core coverage. All states must offer Plan A, but not all of the other plans are available in all states. Rates vary among insurers from $700 a year to $2,000 a year. All 10 must provide core coverage consisting of:

- Part A hospitalization insurance for 61 to 90 days and a lifetime reserve of 91 to 150 days

- 365 hospital days per lifetime paying 100% after Medicare benefits end

- Part B coinsurance for doctor bills
- First three pints of blood

Figure 16.1 provides a breakdown of the 10 plans and their coverage.

> **DID YOU KNOW . . .**
> Want to compare Medigap plans? For $39, Weiss Ratings will provide a list of insurance companies in your area offering Medigap insurance. Included are their rates based on your age and sex. Call (800) 289-9222.

MEDICAID

Medicaid provides medical and health-related services to the poorest people in America by combining funds from the federal government with money from states. The federal government sets minimum guidelines and leaves it to states to administer and set broader requirements for eligibility; the type, amount, duration, and scope of services; and payment.

Medicaid is actually part of the Social Security Act, and has several components, the most well-known of which is the plan that pays for nursing home care. Medicaid's "medically needy" caveat leads middle-class seniors to think they will never qualify. But at $36,000 or more a year for a nursing home stay, a lifetime of savings is quickly wiped out. When savings are gone, your loved one may indeed be medically needy, too.

Medicaid covers doctors and other medical services, as well. Income and asset tests are different for these benefits from those for nursing home care.

To receive federal funds, states must provide Medicaid to people who:

- Receive Aid to Families with Dependent Children (AFDC)
- Receive Supplemental Security Income (SSI), including certain people who are aged, blind, and disabled
- Receive Medicare (under some provisions)

FIGURE 16.1 MEDIGAP PLANS

PLAN	A	B	C	D	E	F	G	H	I	J
Part A deductible		✔	✔	✔	✔	✔		✔	✔	✔
Skilled nursing coinsurance, days 21–100			✔	✔	✔	✔	✔	✔	✔	
Part B deductible			✔			✔				✔
Part B doctor, 80% over Medicare limits							✔			
Part B doctor, 100% over Medicare limits						✔			✔	✔
Foreign travel emergency, pays up to 80% after $250 deductible			✔	✔	✔	✔	✔	✔	✔	✔
Home health care, up to 8 weeks at $40/visit to $1,600/yr. beyond Medicare coverage				✔			✔		✔	✔
Prescription drugs, 50% after $250 deductible, $1,250/yr. limit								✔	✔	
Prescription drugs, 50% after $250 deductible, $3,000/yr. limit										✔
Preventive care: flu shots, cancer tests, diabetes, hearing disorders (up to $120/yr.)					✔					✔

States also may, at their discretion, provide Medicaid to people who:

- Are aged, blind, or disabled with incomes above those requiring mandatory coverage, but below the federal poverty level (medically needy)
- Are institutionalized and have income and resources below specified limits
- Would be eligible if institutionalized, but are receiving care under home and community-based services waivers

Approximately 18 states have income rules for Medicaid recipients.

The "medically needy" provision gives states the authority to extend Medicaid to people who would not ordinarily qualify. When this option is used, such people can spend down, by incurring medical or remedial care expenses to offset their excess income, thus making them more likely to be eligible.

In addition to income, there is a test for assets and resources. The formula used to qualify for Medicaid is complex and varies among states. In general, you may qualify if you receive or are eligible to receive Supplemental Security Income. If you qualify for Medicaid, you are allowed to keep about $584 per month income. This amount varies among states.

With exceptions (of course!), Medicaid pays for physician services, inpatient and outpatient hospital services, nursing home care, medically necessary home health services, transportation to medical services, ambulatory surgery centers, prescriptions, mental health services, chiropractic services, and visual, dental, and hearing services.

If you are age 65 or older and covered by Medicare, it may also pay for your Medicare premium Part B, for deductibles and coinsurance under Part B, and for deductibles under Medicare Part A and coinsurance for nursing home care, podiatry service, and hospice.

If you qualify, Medicaid may even pay medical bills incurred 90 days prior to applying for benefits. However, your health care provider must agree to accept Medicaid reimbursement.

To apply, you will need proof of your income, U.S. citizenship, and age, and medical records if you are disabled. Most states oversee applications and must give you a determination of eligibility within 45 days, or within 60 days if you're disabled.

QUALIFYING FOR MEDICAID NURSING HOME BENEFITS

Medicaid pays almost 45% of nursing home and home health care bills in the United States. In 1995, Medicaid payments for these two services totaled $49 billion for more than 3.4 million recipients.

To qualify for nursing home benefits, a person must have no more than $2,000 in assets. Note that this applies only to the person to be institutionalized, not the spouse. The person in the nursing home is allowed $35 per month to pay for personal needs. Again, these amounts may vary among states.

Certain assets, depending on state law, are exempt from the $2,000 cap. They might include your home, your automobile, some life insurance, funeral and burial plans or accounts, certain annuities, personal property, and possibly some income-producing property.

INCOME LIMITS

In those states where income is an issue, Medicaid considers only income in the name of the applicant, unless the applicant is married. Income in both partners' names is considered to belong to each equally.

The applicant is allowed $35 a month for personal expenses and must spend any remaining income on his or her medical care.

An applicant's spouse is allowed income of about $2,000 a month, though this amount also varies by state. If the spouse's income is more than that, Medicaid will suggest that the spouse contribute 25% of it over $2,019 toward the other partner's medical care, but Medicaid cannot force the spouse to do so.

TRANSFERRING ASSETS

If you or your spouse transfer assets and receive nothing in return, then a penalty period is imposed. Medicaid looks at all transfers in the last 36 months and may look back as much as 60 months (five years) if a trust transfer is involved.

The person applying for Medicaid nursing home coverage is ineligible for a period equal to the value of the transferred asset, divided by the average cost of nursing home services for private patients in his or her community. This amount is determined by the state.

However, a home is exempt from transfer rules if it is transferred to the applicant's spouse, child under age 21 or one who is blind or disabled, brother or sister with an equity interest in the home who resided in the home one year before institutionalization, or son or daughter who resided in the home two years for whom care was provided to keep the person from being institutionalized.

Certain other transfers are also exempt, primarily those that benefit a spouse.

Applying for Medicaid too soon after a transfer can create an eligibility waiting period of 36 months or longer.

In general, a spouse is allowed a Community Spouse Resource Allowance of about $80,000 (in 1998). This amount also varies by state.

> ▼ CAUTION
> In 1997, Congress made it illegal for anyone to counsel or transfer assets for the purpose of qualifying for Medicaid nursing home benefits. The law has been amended to apply only to those who charge a fee for advising or assisting anyone in the transfer of assets, if the transfer creates a penalty period, or if the sole reason for the transfer is to become eligible for Medicaid benefits.

MEDICAID IRREVOCABLE TRUST

Some states that have income caps provide for an *irrevocable trust,* sometimes called a *qualified income trust.* Under such trusts, which must be drawn up by a lawyer, people can put all of their monthly income over the Medicaid income limit into the trust fund. All funds in excess of the income limit go into the trust with the restriction that when the person dies, all the money, up to the amount of Medicaid funds used, goes to the state. Unlike other irrevocable trusts, this type can be amended and terminated under certain conditions.

Getting through the Medicaid maze is grueling. We recommend that, before making asset transfers, you consult an attorney who is well versed in Medicaid rules for your state.

CHAPTER SEVENTEEN

$

Other Types of Insurance: What Can Help and What Is Unnecessary

There is insurance and there is *insurance*. Some types of coverage just take money from us that could be better spent. Other kinds, like health insurance, are unquestionably necessary. Chapter 16 discussed health care coverage. This chapter examines some other common policies your care recipient might have or consider purchasing, in health and other areas.

LONG-TERM CARE (LTC) INSURANCE

LTC insurance is discussed first because it addresses what is probably the most serious concern of elders. Medicare and Medigap cover only some of the costs of skilled care at a nursing facility or in a person's home. But where, many seniors wonder, will the bulk of the money come from for what could one day be a huge expense if institutionalization is required? In 1997 the national average expense for nursing home care was $40,000 a year, according to the United Seniors Health Cooperative, a Washington, D.C.–based not-for-profit organization, which helps older consumers. Those costs are expected to rise to $80,000 by the year 2010, USHC adds.

Increasingly, payment for those expenses is coming from long-term care insurance. More than 120 companies, from health care insurers to investment firms, offer a wide variety of LTC policies. Some cover different levels of care in a nursing home, while others are used to pay for varying skilled care services at home.

The number of LTC policies has more than doubled since 1990, to about four million sold, according to the Health Insurance Association of America, an industry group. HIAA notes that between 400,000 and 500,000 new policies are being sold every year.

For anyone with assets they want to protect, LTC insurance is a wise investment. It will not deplete an inheritance that could otherwise go to nursing home costs, a common concern of the elderly. Similarly, for those who do not want to be dependent on Medicaid one day, this insurance can be a good buy.

Finally, tax laws allow many LTC insurance buyers to deduct at least some of the premiums and mostly eliminate taxes on policy reimbursements.

The most significant disadvantage to purchasing an LTC policy is its cost. This is *expensive* insurance. Some seniors do not have enough assets to warrant the expenditure.

▼ **CAUTION**
If your care recipient is married, both spouses should be covered by LTC insurance so that if a nursing home stay is required by one of them, it won't deplete assets needed by the other. This is an area you (or your loved one) should discuss with a tax advisor, elder law attorney, or financial planner.

LTC insurance seems to be aimed at the middle or upper-middle class—those who will not qualify for Medicaid. The truly wealthy will be wasting money with this purchase; the needy probably cannot afford the premiums and in any event are likely to be eligible for Medicaid.

Here are some points to consider.

- If your care recipient has a family history of Alzheimer's disease or of any disease that requires long-term care, he or she is a good candidate for LTC coverage.

- Women, living longer than men, on the average, with more likelihood of needing nursing home care, may want to look carefully at LTC insurance.

- Age matters in other respects. There is no need to buy LTC insurance when you are too young. The average age at purchase is 67. If your loved one is considering this insurance around that time, fine. But if either of you thinks about buying a policy when you are younger, especially if you are only 50-something, you will pay less for coverage than someone much older, but you will likely be paying that premium for more years than you need. It's when policyholders move through their 70s, 80s, and beyond that the chance that they will require nursing home care increases.

The USHC discourages seniors from considering LTC coverage unless they meet *all* of the following criteria:

- They can count more than $75,000 in assets, or $150,000 per couple (not including a home and car).

- They have an annual retirement income of more than $30,000.

- They have the ability to make premium payments comfortably, without having to make any lifestyle changes.

- They can afford the LTC policy even if premiums increase by 20% to 30% in the future.

Be careful, too, about what is known as *combined triggers*. This means that, in order for benefits to begin, you must have two health problems—for example, cognitive impairment, plus you need help with three out of five tasks of daily living. The better, newer policies offer stand-alone triggers, so a policy will kick in with just one trigger—for example, cognitive impairment alone.

> ▼ CAUTION
>
> Long-term care insurance is sometimes sold door to door or over the phone. That's not a smart way to buy. Contact a local life insurance independent agent or broker.

What is LTC insurance likely to cost? Figure 17.1 will give you a good idea.

As with other types of insurance, the higher the deductible you can afford, the lower your premium will be. Covering 100% of LTC costs through insurance is usually prohibitively expensive. Insuring yourself for coverage for a shorter benefit period, such as two to four years, will be less costly than covering yourself

FIGURE 17.1 TYPICAL LONG-TERM CARE INSURANCE COSTS

Average Annual Premiums for Leading Individual and Group Association Long-Term Care Sellers in 1995*

AGE	BASE PLAN	WITH LIFETIME 5% COMPOUNDED INFLATION PROTECTION ONLY	WITH NONFORFEITURE† BENEFIT ONLY	WITH NONFORFEITURE AND LIFETIME 5% COMPOUNDED INFLATION PROTECTION
\multicolumn{5}{c}{Coverage Amount: $80/40 a Day Nursing Home/Home Health Care}				
50	$ 310	$ 651	$ 451	$ 929
65	817	1,481	1,158	2,149
79	3,353	4,579	4,738	6,800
\multicolumn{5}{c}{Coverage Amount: $100/50 a Day Nursing Home/Home Health Care}				
50	$ 378	$ 798	$ 540	$1,124
65	1,010	1,881	1,395	2,560
79	4,148	5,889	5,676	8,146

*Generally, for a 20-day elimination period (deductible) and four years of coverage.
†Provides some coverage or benefit if policyholder lapses or cannot afford to pay the premium after a certain number of years.

Source: Health Insurance Association of America 1996 LTC Market Survey of 11 companies that accounted for approximately 80% of individual and group policies nationwide.

for the rest of your life. Although any nursing home administrator can point out residents who have been in that facility for several years, most nursing home stays are for less than three years.

DID YOU KNOW . . .
Because of competition in the field, rates for LTC insurance have dropped by around 30% in the last few years, so if your loved one has an old policy you should reevaluate it.

You can call just about any life insurance company and inquire about LTC insurance. Figure 17.2 will help you to ask the right questions of agents or brokers.

Thanks to legislation passed in 1992, free long-term care insurance counseling is available in every area of the country. Call your (or your loved one's) local agency on aging or state insurance department to find the nearest office.

There are additional resources that can help you with information about this important issue:

FIGURE 17.2 COMPARING LTC POLICIES

Here are some questions to ask companies offering LTC insurance and some points for comparison:

- Are benefits adjusted for inflation? (If not, the dollar amount you purchase today may amount to little in 10 to 20 years.)
- How much are the daily benefits? (Then determine how much you may have to pay out of pocket and how you will pay for it.)
- What are the policy restrictions and the waiting period to use benefits?
- Which types of facilities are included and excluded?
- How long do the benefits last? Number of days? Consecutive years?
- What is excluded from coverage?
- How much does the premium cost? What about increases?
- What is the insurance company's rating? (There is an explanation of these ratings in Chapter 15.)
- Is there a nonforfeiture benefit so that you can get something back if you cancel the policy?

- "Before You Buy: A Guide to Long-Term Care Insurance" is a free pamphlet from the American Association of Retired Persons. Write AARP Fulfillment, 601 E Street NW, Washington, DC 20049.

- The book, *Long-Term Care: A Dollar and Sense Guide,* is available for $15 from United Seniors Health Cooperative, 1331 H Street NW, Suite 500, Washington, DC 20005.

- "A Guide to Long-Term Care Insurance" is a free booklet offered by the Health Insurance Association of America. Call toll free (888) 844-2782.

- Many state insurance departments offer free printed material on LTC insurance.

DID YOU KNOW . . .
In most states, if you change your mind after purchasing LTC insurance, you have 30 days to cancel that policy.

AN ELDER'S LIFE INSURANCE

Several chapters in this book have talked about life insurance. Here we are discussing whether your care recipient needs this coverage.

The care recipient *may* want to drop life insurance to save on premiums. If he or she owns a home free and clear, has suitable health care coverage, and is able to live day to day in reasonable comfort, life insurance might not be necessary. A financial planner can advise what's best here. For example, keep in mind that, although your care recipient will save on premiums, if the person should want to reapply for coverage and by then is in poor health, he or she could be considered uninsurable.

Here is a suggestion. If your relative has a cash value or whole life insurance policy, which, as you recall from Chapter 11, includes a savings account feature, you can send a copy of that policy to the Insurance Group of the Consumer Federation of America. The group will analyze the person's rate of return and offer an idea of what he or she would have to earn from investments to do better than that figure. The service costs $40. Call CFA at (202) 387-0087.

VIATICAL SETTLEMENT

This is not an insurance policy, but rather a payout on a term life insurance policy that your loved one might hold.

The settlement is for those with terminal, or even chronic, illnesses. It works like this: A company purchases an ailing person's life insurance policy for a portion of its face value, which is usually around 70%. The percentage varies according to the length of time the person is expected to live. For example, someone with a life expectancy of two years or less (naturally, a doctor's opinion is sought) might receive 60% on a policy; someone who presumably has less than six months to live might recoup 80%. The individual applying for the settlement gets the money, and the viatical company either holds the policy and takes over premiums, collecting on the policy when that individual dies, or sells the policy to an investor who does that.

Viatical (the word comes from the Latin meaning "provisions for a journey") settlements have become quite prominent in the last decade or so. They have proved particularly effective in providing financial support for AIDS sufferers but, as mentioned above, can be used with other illnesses.

Regulations dealing with viatical companies, issued by the National Association of Insurance Commissioners, have been adopted in some form in several states. Call your loved one's state insurance department to see if that office has some guidelines for viatical settlements.

Your relative (or you acting for the person) should get bids from at least three viatical companies. You can find them and learn more about this method of increasing income by calling the Viatical Association of America at (800) 842-9811.

———▼▼▼———

Those who have never been ill are incapable of
real sympathy for a great many misfortunes.
Andre Gide, JOURNALS *(1930)*

———▲▲▲———

MORTGAGE INSURANCE

It is not likely that your care recipient has mortgage insurance.
This is often taken out by those with young families, to provide
for a mortgage payoff in the event of the wage earner's death.
Your loved one may have either no mortgage or only a small balance. Still, perhaps in a flurry of insuring against *any* eventuality,
your relative might talk about signing up for this protection or
may have already done so.

It is unnecessary. Its proceeds can only pay off a mortgage,
going to a lender, whereas a life insurance policy, which your relative probably already has, can be used for anything, including
paying off a home loan. Skip mortgage insurance.

> ▼ **CAUTION**
> Don't confuse mortgage insurance with *private mort-*
> *gage insurance* (PMI), which mortgage lenders usually
> require of home buyers making a low down payment.

CANCER INSURANCE

This is another policy your care recipient doesn't need. Cancer,
or "dread disease," insurance, which can cover other specified
ailments, is usually a duplication of existing health care coverage. It also is restrictive in what it allows a policyholder to claim,
with limited benefits. Indeed, some states have banned these
policies from being sold, citing too few economic benefits.

Nobody can say with certainty that they are going to contract a
particular disease. If your loved one is 65 or over, your best bet is
Medicare plus a good Medigap policy (see Chapter 16). Long-
term care insurance is another option.

CHAPTER EIGHTEEN

$

Your Loved One's Estate Plan

his is certainly a delicate area. It's difficult enough to bring up a senior's finances, particularly if the conversation is between parent and child. Having to raise issues such as whether a parent has a will seems a little self-serving. In ruder terms, it could be considered nosy and even greedy. If you are caring for a more distant relative or a friend, everything in that area could be considered none of your business.

Still, you know how important these documents can be for you in *your* life. They become even more so for an elder, who may be on the brink of needing some of the benefits such papers offer. Not having them is going to cause confusion and consternation for family members. Also, your care recipient may not have his or her wishes carried out because they are not down in black and white in a valid legal document.

You can handle the topics in this area of your loved one's life gingerly and diplomatically, while still accomplishing what needs to be done.

IF YOUR CARE RECIPIENT IS ABLE TO HANDLE HIS OR HER OWN AFFAIRS

It is easy to slip into a conversation about these topics if you have just had some of those instruments drawn up yourself—a will, for example.

"I just had my will done, Mom," you might say. "Figured I should. You know, it got me thinking . . . I didn't realize I had so many assets and so many decisions to make about them. You have a will, don't you?" That could lead to a discussion between you. The same technique can be used for durable power of attorney and health care proxy.

If the answer is yes when you ask about these documents, ask your parent where they are kept. Again, it might be an easier question for your loved one to answer if you volunteer where you have filed *your* will, durable power of attorney, and so on.

> **▼? DID YOU KNOW . . .**
> If aware of what he or she is doing, your care recipient can make out a will, health care proxy, or the like even if the person has been diagnosed with Alzheimer's but is in the early stages of that disease.

If you don't have the sort of relationship with your loved one that lends itself to this kind of conversation, you might ask a friend or associate to ask a few questions for you. Seniors often listen to professionals in their lives, or even strangers, while they are resistant to taking family members' or friends' advice. You might ask the loved one's doctor to raise the issue of a health care proxy. To avoid causing alarm, the doctor could mention that this is standard procedure with senior patients. Your parent's accountant could broach the subject of a will when discussing estate taxes or any new change in the tax law that could affect current savings or assets to be bequeathed. A geriatric care manager may help here, too. A financial planner will almost certainly ask your parent if he or she has all of these appropriate papers.

A *health care power of attorney* for an ailing senior can be vitally important. In this situation your conversation might turn to a neighbor or a friend who died, how the family didn't know the person's wishes, the children bickered about medical decisions, and the whole thing was a complicated, terrible business. But who knew what the deceased would have wanted? There was no legal document that could give everyone some direction.

▼▼▼

The first wealth is health.
Ralph Waldo Emerson,
"The Conduct of Life" (1860)

▲▲▲

Asking a parent about a durable power of attorney can be tricky. None of us want to think about the likelihood of losing control over our lives or losing our ability to write a check or make decisions we think of as everyday and relatively simple. While loss of control may be a distant consideration for you, it is probably a very real possibility for your aging relative and is likely to be more than an occasional thought. In this case, too, if you can't come up with a way of insinuating it comfortably into a conversation, a professional might be able to help.

The moment your parent sees the validity of having these documents, follow up immediately with an offer of assistance. Make an appointment with a lawyer for the soonest possible date.

Don't give up, though, if your parent doesn't want to talk about such issues and waves you away. Keep raising the subject. It may take time for your loved one to see the wisdom of preparing these documents.

Since your care recipient is mentally agile, he or she is no doubt able to keep up with the savings and investment part of the estate plan. However, there is another addition to that file that may be under consideration.

PREPAYING A FUNERAL

This has become quite popular in recent years, particularly with seniors. You don't just plan your funeral, you pay for it—*right now.* This is not financially sound, a point you will want to convey to your loved one. Why withdraw from savings that are earning interest the $5,000 to $7,500 or more that a funeral would cost, only to give it to a cemetery or funeral home, which can then invest and earn interest? Nevertheless, some seniors feel better having paid for a funeral and think, too, they are saving their heirs the time and expense of doing so.

High-pressure sales tactics to buy the best (translation: most expensive) of everything are sometimes used in preneed sales. These sales may not be regulated by federal law, although some states have such statutes on the books. So this is an area that could be full of land mines for your relative. However, since the advanced payment plan business is increasing by some 20% a year, look for more stringent regulation, especially since older Americans are involved.

It does make sense to *plan* a funeral, if that interests your care recipient. Purchasing a cemetery plot or deciding on cremation, planning the ceremony, and so on, are fine. Such foresight can help family members down the road, and it does not involve a sizable and unnecessary expenditure of money. Such planning carries out your loved one's specific wishes, too. Sound advice is therefore to plan, yes; to prepay, no. Chapter 19 offers more detail about funerals.

IF YOUR RELATIVE IS UNABLE TO DISCUSS IMPORTANT PAPERS

Perhaps your loved one is not able to make any decisions. It can happen quickly, as with a stroke, or it may be gradual, as with forms of dementia. In any event, asking the person about estate-related matters is out of the question.

What happens now?

If the loved one has a durable power of attorney, you or whoever the person has designated can make financial and other decisions (based on what is in that document) for the person. Similarly, if the loved one has a health care proxy, that individual can step in with health-related matters.

However, what if your loved one has neither?

THE ISSUE OF GUARDIANSHIP

In lieu of a valid durable power of attorney or health care power of attorney, your loved one will need a court-appointed guardian.

This is not the best possible way to handle the person's affairs, since it is then up to the state to appoint the guardian and it could be someone the loved one would not want acting in that capacity.

You or another family member petition the court (usually probate or surrogate's court, but it could be a county or circuit court) to appoint a guardian. The guardian is a person with the power and duty to make decisions about the personal and/or financial affairs of your loved one. A judge will decide who is going to serve in that capacity. The law varies from state to state, although generally speaking, courts won't name anyone who has financial or personal interests that conflict with those of the ward. For example, someone who is a creditor of the person in need of a guardian is not likely to be named. Judges can deny any appointment they deem not in the best interest of the ward.

Usually, but not always, the guardian role will go to the nearest relative in this order: spouse first, then children, and then other relatives. If there are no relatives, a friend will be considered. If that is not possible either, the judge will appoint someone (but not a friend of that judge).

> **DID YOU KNOW . . .**
> Some states allow residents to name guardians in advance, looking ahead to the time when that role may become necessary. This can be done by a separate document or as part of a power of attorney. Ask your lawyer how it works in your state, if it is permitted.

Guardianship laws vary geographically. What a guardian can and cannot do is defined by the law in that particular jurisdiction. Terms are sometimes different, too. In some jurisdictions a *guardian* will handle your loved one's personal affairs, while a *conservator* might be appointed for business and financial matters. The term that applies to your mother could be *ward,* or it might be *legally incapacitated person.*

Among a guardian's powers might be the right to make a nursing home placement for a ward; to apply for government benefits; to decide where the ward is to live; to ensure that food, clothing, and other day-to-day needs are met; and even to initiate divorce or separation proceedings if the guardian thinks that is in the best interest of the ward.

If the guardian is given control over financial matters, this can include handling assets from managing property to renting or selling an apartment or home, receiving income, and controlling money of the incapacitated person.

The notion of incapacity is constantly evolving, as we live longer and definitions of physical and mental illness continue to change as well. In some states with older guardianship statutes on the books, the requirement is of a particular physical or mental condition, as well as the inability, resulting from that condition, to manage one's personal or financial affairs. Newer laws set different criteria. They require the inability of the ward to perform and a lack of understanding of the consequences of one's actions.

Some forms of guardianship are more restrictive than others, too. The trend these days has been to set the guardian's powers to the functional limitations of the ward, which keeps in mind the ward's decision-making capacity and his or her rights. Sometimes a *limited guardianship* is put into place, which curbs some of the guardian's rights and responsibilities, while retaining some important autonomy for the ward.

It is apparent how making such personal and far-reaching judgments for a person who cannot do it for him- or herself calls for just the right person, someone close enough to know the person's wishes—someone caring and honest, too, in carrying out those wishes and other responsibilities of the guardianship role. That is not necessarily the individual a judge will name.

Guardianship is sometimes unavoidable—there just has not been time to make better arrangements. However, if your loved one *can* make decisions, the best alternative to having a state-appointed guardian is planning ahead. That means having a valid revocable living trust or a power of attorney or health care proxy.

▼ **CAUTION**
An important consideration of guardianship is cost. There are fees attached to court filings, the guardian's bond, and other expenses, which could amount to several thousand dollars over the life of the person needing guardianship. That's another good reason to plan so that guardianship is avoided.

HELPING YOUR PARENT PREPARE A WILL AND RELATED DOCUMENTS

You can refer to Chapter 10 for explanations of these documents and what having them drawn up entails. Of course, if you have just had them done for yourself, your own experience is an even better aid to your parent.

By all means call on a lawyer for help here. Your loved one may want to raise age-related issues (or the attorney will bring them up) that might not concern you if you are not a contemporary, such as potential nursing home costs as they could affect an estate's assets.

WHERE ARE THESE DOCUMENTS KEPT?

As suggested earlier in this chapter, during discussions of a will, durable power of attorney, and the like, try to learn from your loved one where he or she keeps these documents or intends to keep them after they have been drawn up. If they are kept in a bank safe deposit box (not wise, as mentioned in Chapter 10), find out, if you can, at which financial institution it is located. If the documents are with the person's lawyer, ask who that is. The more information you can gather, the better, because you may need it one day.

While it is certainly true that some seniors do not want to do this advance planning and others will not want to talk with you about it if they have done it, there are other situations where a

FIGURE 18.1 IN AN EMERGENCY

If your relative becomes mentally incapacitated, whether for a temporary period of time or with no hope for recovery, you will need the following information:

- The name and phone number of the person's physician
- The extent of the person's health care coverage
- If they exist, the person's durable power of attorney and health care power of attorney (or living will)
- Preparation, if it becomes necessary, for a guardianship petition if the person has no legal proxy papers
- The key to the person's home, if you do not already have it
- A list of when mortgage or rent, utilities, and/or telephone payments are due
- The person's wishes regarding care for any pet(s)

loved one will, sometimes without even being asked, hand a child or other family member a list of all the information—names, addresses, account numbers, and so on—he or she will need in the event of an emergency. (See Figure 18.1.) Maybe you'll be one of those fortunate caregivers!

CHAPTER NINETEEN

$

End-of-Life Decisions

W hen the end is near, many decisions must be made. Hopefully, your loved one has made important decisions ahead of time or, at the least, let his or her wishes be known. Chapter 18 discussed the instruments by which some of these decisions can be made, including wills and advance directives. Other decisions include choosing between burial or cremation and myriad choices that come with either selection.

Death often comes swiftly, when we least expect it, but sometimes it is foretold by a physician well in advance. The latter is often true for people dying from cancer or similar diseases.

HOSPICE CARE

When you know a person's disease is terminal and time is limited, you might consider hospice care.

Hospice is a special type of care—a philosophy, really—designed for people who have six months or less to live, and their families. The hospice philosophy is the concept of "a good death," one as free from pain and worry as possible. Hospice care is palliative or comfort-oriented care.

The hospice concept was started in England in the 1960s by Dr. Cicely Saunders and made its way to the states about 10 years later. Nonprofit hospices have become a burgeoning industry, with over 2,400 organizations providing service in most cities and towns in a vast number of countries.

Hospice care neither prolongs nor shortens life. Rather, a professional, hospice-trained team strives to keep the patient comfortable and relatively pain free. Hospice workers and volunteers provide physical, emotional, psychological, and spiritual care. In addition, both patients and their families are encouraged to participate in caregiving decisions.

Although the number of people opting for hospice care increased more than 100% between 1984 and 1994, there are those who do not embrace the entire philosophy. The hospice attitude is positive, and part of the care centers on family and faith. People estranged from their families or who don't care to have them around, or people who are agnostic or atheist may not find the hospice philosophy acceptable. Also, like any other organization or service, there are good and bad providers and caretakers. Overall, families who have used hospice care like the comprehensive approach that embraces dying in your own home instead of in an institution. Such an approach also cuts down considerably on end-of-life health care costs—and this may be important to your loved one.

A hospice team comprises:

- *A doctor,* who diagnoses the patient's illness as terminal before hospice care can begin. This may be the patient's doctor or a doctor within the hospice organization.

- *A registered nurse,* who provides medical care, such as giving medications, administering intravenous therapy, or caring for wounds.

- *A social worker,* who is trained to counsel the ill person and the family in a variety of matters, including funeral arrangements, advance directives, Social Security benefits, and even finances.

- *A homemaker,* who may help with cooking, cleaning, or other household chores.

- *A clergy member,* either nondenominational or of the family's faith.

- *Volunteers,* who provide a respite for family members or help in other ways.

Hospice care most often is provided in the patient's or a family member's home. Some hospices have their own facilities, and there is a growing trend toward providing hospice care in nursing homes and other facilities. The hospice team is not present 24 hours a day, but certain team members are on call at all times, including holidays.

▼? DID YOU KNOW . . .
In medieval times, *hospice* meant "a place of shelter and rest" for weary or sick travelers returning from pilgrimages. The word springs from the Latin *hospitium,* meaning "guest house."

PAYING FOR HOSPICE CARE

Medicare most often pays for hospice care. This stands to reason since about 90% of all hospice patients are age 65 or older. Over two thirds of the states also pay for hospice care under Medicaid programs. A growing number of health insurance companies, including HMOs, also cover hospice care. But the hospice philosophy is based on need, not ability to pay, so no one is turned away.

Hospice organizations may receive city, state, and federal grants to cover care for those who are unable to pay, and many are supported by companies and other organizations in their communities through grants and fund-raising events. Individuals and families who have benefited from hospice care may also give donations.

Most insurers, including Medicare, require that patients elect to forgo traditional medical treatment to receive limited hospice care for the terminal illness. However, if the patient requires treatment for a condition not related to the terminal illness, most insurers, Medicare included, will pay for traditional medical care for the unrelated condition.

Medicare requires a small copayment for prescribed drugs and respite care. Other than that, Medicare covers all the costs of hospice care, including:

- Physician and nursing services
- Prescribed medications, including those to alleviate and manage pain
- Physical, occupational, and speech therapies
- Home health aide and homemaker services
- Short-term inpatient care when medically necessary
- Respite care
- Social services that are medically oriented
- Counseling with dietitians and clergy
- Continuous care during periods of crisis
- Bereavement services

For more information on hospice care, contact the National Hospice Organization, 1901 North Moore St., Suite 901, Arlington, VA 22209, (703) 243-5900, or the toll-free hot line at (800) 658-8898.

ARRANGING THE FUNERAL— WHOSE PREFERENCE?

Unbelievable as it may sound, many adult children, spouses, or other family members may not know what a person's wishes are for his or her funeral. A person who dies *intestate* (the legal term for being without a will) or a family that has never discussed death may be totally in the dark. This is often the case, too, when the deceased is a child or someone in his or her 20s or 30s.

Usually the most immediate family member—the spouse or parent(s)—makes the decisions. But even then trouble can arise when extended families are involved. A woman who was married 20 years to one man, divorced him, then died within a short time of remarrying, is a perfect example. She did not leave a will and had not yet discussed her wishes with the new spouse. The former husband was the only one who knew what her wishes were. Those wishes conflicted with the new spouse's.

Most states recognize that the current spouse makes the decisions. That's the legal solution, but not necessarily the emotional one. The family's religion and mores may also be involved. And remember that funerals are for the living, not the dead. Everything you do is to comfort those who are still alive and who must cope with their grief and pain.

One family was almost torn apart when the mother wanted to cremate her adult child who had died unexpectedly. The child had no will and had never discussed death. The mother, who was divorced from the child's father, chose cremation. The rest of the family, who didn't believe in cremation, was aghast. The child's father protested as well, claiming he had a right to decide, which legally he did. The mother solved the problem by communicating with the family.

Savvy consumers compare prices on most major purchases, but when it comes to funerals, the search usually ends at one funeral home. That's easy to understand under the circumstances of sudden death. Unless your loved one has prearranged his or her own funeral, the death of a loved one is a difficult time to be making major financial decisions. The problem begins with emotional turmoil.

PLANNING THE FUNERAL

When a family member dies, even if the death was imminent, loved ones exhibit shock, disbelief, and a host of other emotions. There are countless details to contend with, including notifying family members and friends; making arrangements for their travel and arrival; dealing with doctors, hospitals, emergency personnel, police, newspaper reporters, and others, depending on the circumstances of the death. When you add funeral arrangements to a world suddenly turned upside down, stress is inevitable.

The first decision is whether the person should be buried or cremated. The wishes, religion, and family choices of the deceased will help you make this decision. If the choice is for burial, as nearly 80% of all choices are, here is what you need to know.

BURIAL SERVICES AND COSTS

First you will have to choose a funeral home. In many cities this is limited to one or two choices as the industry consolidates and conglomerates purchase family-run homes. The choice is often based on input from friends or family members. Religious preference may also play a role; for example, when you thumb through the telephone directory, "Catholic Funeral Home" may catch your eye.

The home's funeral director will ascertain your wishes and provide guidance. This is also where you need to be on your toes. A funeral today typically costs between $5,000 and $15,000, though you can spend more and sometimes less.

Take along a strong family member or friend, who can help you make commonsense—not emotional—decisions. Ask a lot of questions. Funeral homes charge for every service rendered, even in a "complete burial package." If a package is offered, ask what it includes and be sure each item is spelled out in the contract.

Charges begin with a professional service fee that averaged right at $1,000 nationwide in 1996, according to the National Funeral Directors' Association. This fee essentially is a cover charge for using the home's services. Some funeral homes set this fee high and charge less for other services, while others do just the opposite. Again, find out what is included in this charge.

The next charge you may encounter, about $125, is for picking up the body from the hospital, home, or airport, if the body is shipped from one state to another. (Airlines charge a hefty price for shipping a body and the cost is accompanied by strict rules. The amount varies by distance, e.g., California to Florida versus New York to Ohio.) Also, the funeral home in the state from which the body is shipped will charge for picking up the body, placing it in a casket, and taking it to the airport.

If there is to be a viewing, the body will have to be embalmed, a process that preserves the body for a limited period of time. Expect to pay about $350 for this service and perhaps another $100 or so to dress the body, prepare the hair, and add makeup. Most states do not require embalming, except when the body is shipped across state lines, so if you don't plan a viewing, make sure you don't pay for embalming.

If you plan a viewing, there may be a charge for a viewing room (a private room set aside at the funeral home), unless this cost is incorporated into the service fee. This can run about $300. Some religions require that a family member stay with the body at all times. If this is true in your case, you might have to pay extra charges for this as well, as viewing rooms are reused constantly during the day and evening.

The most expensive charge by far is for the casket and possibly a liner. Caskets are constructed from various woods and metals and can be elaborate or plain, both inside and out. A casket can be purchased from the funeral home, from a cemetery, or even from a specialty discount store for caskets, which are growing in numbers. Expect to pay between $15,000 and $18,000 for a bronze casket; about $2,000 for oak; and between $400 and $500 for a cloth-covered casket. A sealing gasket (which offers no additional protection) can add about $1,000 more to the cost.

Few states require a grave liner or concrete vault, which is a box placed in the ground into which the casket is laid. You'll pay about $300 for a liner and about $600 for a vault. Some cemeteries require a liner, which keeps the ground from settling after burial, because it reduces their upkeep of the grounds.

You may pay for a hearse to carry the body to the cemetery and perhaps a limousine or special car for family members. Also, there may be charges for a police escort for the funeral party. Figure $200 for the hearse and driver, $100 for a limo, and $100 more or less for a police escort. Some funeral homes also charge for a car or van to carry flowers to the cemetery. Add another $75 for this.

A funeral service can be performed at a church or at the funeral home. If you are a member of the church or synagogue, you may be able to get the pastor, rabbi, or priest to give the eulogy, either at the church or in another facility. Most churches and clergy do not charge for this service, but may gratefully accept a donation. When the service is held at the funeral home, add another couple of hundred dollars to the bill. Watch out for extra charges for parking and other services.

Finally, there is a charge for the cemetery plot. Many people have already purchased a plot earlier in life. Some families purchase plots for all family members, with an extra one or two for children not yet born. If your family or loved one has not done so, you will have to purchase one now.

Cemetery plots range from $750 to $1,500. The cost usually covers only the 6½-foot by 4-foot piece of ground to be dug for the grave. The price may also include maintenance. When considering a cemetery, find out what its rules and regulations are. Some are quite strict about the type and size of headstone or monument, and this could add to your costs. Some spell out grave visitation rules and when flowers or other memorials may be placed, as well as when they must be removed. Some include overall maintenance; others charge a monthly fee. Some also hold special services throughout the year, for example, on holidays such as Christmas or Memorial Day. Others place identical wreaths or flowers on all the graves at certain times of the year. Limits may be placed on whether you may have silk or cut flowers or may plant trees and shrubs. Some cemeteries cater to a particular religion or class, such as military cemeteries.

The cemetery normally charges a fee for opening and/or closing the grave, which includes digging the hole. This cost averages $500 to $800 on weekdays, more on weekends. If the cemetery provides chairs and a tent for a graveside service, you may also pay for these.

Finally, you will want a headstone to mark the grave. Like caskets, headstones can be elaborate creations or monuments or as simple as a small marker with the person's name and dates of birth and death. Military cemeteries provide free grave markers, because they must be of a uniform size and shape. Headstones are made from granite or other hard stones and are often engraved with text and pictures. They can also be etched with a likeness of the deceased. Some come with a holder for flowers or a waterproof pocket in which a photograph can be inserted. You can also purchase a grave cover, usually a flat granite piece that covers the entire grave. This also can be etched, and the headstone usually sits at the head (hence the name). Figure on paying $500 to $1,000 for headstones and markers.

CREMATION

Cremation used to be a fairly simple way to dispose of a body, but people who choose cremation often include some of the formalities associated with burial. When a body is cremated, it is placed in an inexpensive wooden casket and taken to a crematorium, where it is burned at high heat.

> **CAUTION**
> Be sure all jewelry is removed from a loved one's body after death and before the body is sent for cremation. Most contracts allow the crematorium to dispose of jewelry left on the body *as they see fit.*

Most cities have only one crematorium, so all funeral homes and cremation companies use the same site. While some crematoriums may burn just one body at a time, some burn several bodies at the same time, but separately, so that the ashes may be collected and given to the family, if that is their wish.

Crematoriums will not allow a person with a mechanical or radioactive device, such as a pacemaker or an implant, to be cremated unless written permission is given allowing the removal of the device.

Families may opt to purchase an urn or box in which to keep the ashes. Like miniature caskets, they come in a wide range of types and sizes. Look for one with a lining that can be sealed. An urn is sealed with glue to keep it from being accidentally dropped and having its contents spilled.

Ashes can be placed in specially designed niches in a cemetery, or they can be scattered in a place designated by the deceased or where the loved one thinks appropriate. This may be at sea, in a river or lake that was the deceased's favorite vacation or fishing spot, or perhaps in a rose garden at home.

You can request that the ashes be divided into several boxes for multiple family members. You may also save some and scatter others. Ashes may even be buried at the grave of another loved one, although, again, you must abide by cemetery rules.

Even with a cremation, some families opt for a viewing and a service. If you do, the same charges will apply as with a funeral—or they may be even higher.

Another alternative is a memorial service, which can be held at a place of your choice, including your home. For example, the friends and family of a sailor who died of a heart attack while living on his sailboat held a memorial service a week after the cremation on the dock where he kept his boat.

Some religions, such as Hindu, require or embrace cremation. Certain rites must be performed in combination with the cremation. For instance, some Hindu sects require the eldest son to push the casket containing his father into the crematory fire. Some crematories may not permit this.

DIRECT BURIAL OR CREMATION

If expenses are a concern with either burial or cremation, consider direct services. A direct burial is the no-frills way of being put in the ground. The body goes from place of death to the cemetery without any fanfare. The price averages about $2,000. Direct cremation is even less expensive, about $700 is the national average. The price usually includes transport of the body to the crematorium, disposal of the ashes, an obituary, and a death certificate.

WRITING MEMORIAL CARDS
AND THE OBITUARY

Both memorial cards and an obituary will most likely mean additional costs. Memorial cards, which commemorate the deceased's death, may contain a prayer or poem on one side and information on the other, such as the person's full name, age, date of birth, date of death, and any other information that is pertinent. These can be purchased from the funeral home (about $25 for 100) and sometimes from the cemetery. You may also purchase pretty cards that are blank inside from a card, gift, or stationery shop and have a printer print the insides.

Obituaries are placed in newspapers at least a day before the visitation, memorial service, or funeral is held. They alert friends and family of the person's death, giving them a chance to call, visit, or send flowers. Some newspapers do not charge for an obituary, but allow "just the facts" free. Others charge per line, the same as classified advertising, but at a much higher rate. Most obituaries are placed by the funeral home and are written with the family's assistance. In fact, some newspapers may not permit individuals to place the obituary, and with good reason: That opens the door for pranksters to report the death of someone very much alive. When the funeral home places the paid obituary, it usually charges a markup—up to 50%—to the customer. Always ask the cost of the obituary and, if possible, write it yourself. When a funeral home is making money by the line, you'll find lots of superfluous information.

All you really need in an obituary is the deceased's full name, age (if you wish), and cause of death (if you wish), along with information on where, when, and what time visitation or services will be held. Some people use this space to request that flowers not be sent or that donations be made to a particular charity in lieu of flowers. You also may include the names of family members left behind, although in some large or extended families, this can quickly get out of hand.

PAYING FOR SERVICES

Unless your loved one has prepaid his or her funeral expenses, you most likely will cover the cost of the funeral with proceeds from life insurance or from the estate. Life insurance proceeds usually take about 30 days to receive and an estate may take six months or more to settle.

Don't be pressured into paying for the funeral in advance. Almost all funeral homes require a deposit, with the balance due within 30 days. Cremation services may have to be paid for in advance.

In every case, the heirs or family members are required to sign a contract, an agreement to pay for the services.

DID YOU KNOW . . .
Social Security pays a beneficiary's estate a lump-sum death benefit of $255.

MILITARY VETERAN DEATH BENEFITS

Men and women who served four years or more in any branch of the military and received an honorable discharge are eligible for many benefits at the veteran's death.

To apply for benefits, you will need the following documents, as they apply:

- Marriage certificate for a surviving spouse or children
- Death certificate if the veteran did not die in a VA medical facility
- Children's birth certificates for children's benefits
- Veteran's birth certificate for parents
- DD-214 (discharge papers)

Benefits available to veterans' families include burial in a national cemetery, headstones and grave markers, burial flags, reimbursed burial expenses, and pensions. To be eligible, a veteran must have been honorably discharged or separated from the service and must have completed his or her period of service; spouses and children qualify under certain conditions.

Where space is available, veterans qualify for a gravesite at one of 114 national cemeteries. A gravesite also is provided for the veteran's spouse and children. The free gravesite includes the costs of opening and closing the grave, perpetual care, headstones, and a marker. Burial may also be provided at state veteran cemeteries; rules differ by state.

Inscribed headstones and markers are provided to veterans for unmarked graves anywhere in the world. They come in bronze, marble, and granite, and can be flat or upright. Niche markers for urns also are available. Costs are inclusive for burial at national or state veterans cemeteries. At private cemeteries, spouses and children are not eligible for a free marker. Also, families pay to have the veteran's marker placed on the grave.

DID YOU KNOW . . .
Friends and relatives of honorably discharged, deceased veterans can receive a certificate signed by the president of the United States recognizing the veteran's service to the country. Apply at local VA offices and bring the DD-214.

The VA provides, at no cost, an American flag to drape over a veteran's casket. Following the funeral, the flag is folded and given to the next of kin. Flags can be picked up at VA regional offices, national cemeteries, and post offices, or the funeral home may do this for you.

If a veteran dies as the result of a service-connected problem, the VA will reimburse up to $1,500 in burial expenses and pay the cost of transporting the remains. It also will pay an additional $150 for a burial plot in a private cemetery.

In addition to burial expenses, the VA has several programs that pay certain spouses and dependents lump-sum and monthly benefits, as well as education benefits. Check with a VA counselor for qualification criteria.

> ▼**DID YOU KNOW . . .**
> Family members of deceased veterans who are buried or commemorated overseas can receive a free passport to visit the sites. For more information, contact the American Battle Monuments Commission, Room 5127, Pulaski Building, 20 Massachusetts Avenue NW, Washington, DC 20314.

DEATH CERTIFICATES

After someone dies, you will need death certificates to prove that he or she has passed away. In most cases, the funeral home or company handling the cremation will arrange for these. Death certificates are issued by a state's Bureau of Vital Statistics or a similar agency. Most charge $3 to $5 for the first, as well as for additional, certificates. A death certificate normally has a raised seal, proving its authenticity.

FIGURE 19.1 FUNERAL CHECKLIST

	BURIAL	CREMATION
Funeral home/provider		
Cemetery/plot location		
Headstone/inscription		
Casket or urn		
Vault or crypt		
Clothing for deceased		
Scripture selections		
Clergy		
Music/musician		
Place of service		
Flowers or donations		
Name of charity		
Obituary		
Pallbearers		
Information for eulogy		
Family transportation		

You will need five or more original death certificates. Banks, life insurance companies, government agencies, and a host of other companies will each require one in order for you to handle the deceased person's affairs. Some may accept a copy if they also see the original, and others may simply accept a copy. You will need to ask each company which it prefers.

Figure 19.1 is a checklist of items you will need to consider when planning a funeral.

CHAPTER TWENTY

$

It's Free!
(or at Least Low Cost)

As you have learned from reading through this book, many companies and organizations offer free or reduced-rate publications, products, and services. Most free publications are available from national organizations or groups. At the local and state level you will certainly find a whole lot more. Remember, part of your job in finding resources for you or a loved one is seeking out the things that can help both of you.

We've arranged this chapter by category: publications, services, and products. A publication, of course, is something that you read—a book, pamphlet, or brochure. In the services section you'll find indirect assistance, such as a group that offers referrals or provides help directly. And the products section includes things that are tangible, such as hearing aids or prescriptions. Sometimes these categories overlap, but we'll stick to this format as much as possible. You will, however, find multiple listings for certain providers.

Each category listing is in alphabetical order. If a few entries look familiar, you may have read about them in preceding chapters as they applied to a particular topic. All of these resources are free unless otherwise noted.

PUBLICATIONS

ACCOUNTING

American Institute of Certified Public Accountants
(800) 999-9256; www.aicpa.org
Personal financial specialist designation information for certain members.

AGING

National Institute on Aging Information Center
(800) 222-2225
List of publications; wide body of resources.

ALZHEIMER'S DISEASE

Alzheimer's Disease Education and Referral Center
(800) 438-4380
Booklets and pamphlets on disease research and caregiver issues. Nominal cost for some.

CAREGIVER ASSOCIATIONS

Children of Aging Parents
(215) 945-6900 or (800) 227-7294
Membership fee of $20 covers bimonthly newsletter, pamphlets.

National Family Caregiver Alliance
425 Bush St. #500
San Francisco, CA 94108
(415) 434-3388
info@caregiver.org
Membership group for caregivers. Printed material.

ELDER LAW

National Academy of Elder Law Attorneys
(520) 881-4005
Brochure: "Questions and Answers When Looking for an Elder Law Attorney," $25.

ESTATE PLANNING

American College of Trust and Estate Counsel
(310) 398-1888; www.actec.org
List of member lawyers skilled in estate planning in your area.

FINANCIAL PLANNING

Institute of Certified Financial Planners
(800) 282-7526; www.icfp.org
Pamphlets.

International Association for Financial Planning
(888) 806-PLAN; www.iafp.org
Fact sheets and brochures.

National Association of Personal Financial Advisors
(888) 333-6659; www.napfa.org
List of fee-only planners.

Securities and Exchange Commission
(800) 732-0330; www.sec.gov
Educational materials on planners.

Certified Financial Planner Board of Standards
(888) 237-6275; www.cfp-board.org
Printed material.

HOME CARE

Joint Commission on the Accreditation of Healthcare Organizations
1 Renaissance Blvd.
Oakbrook Terrace, IL 60181
(630) 916-5800
$30 fee for reports on home health care agencies.

National Association for Home Care
228 7th St. SE
Washington, DC 20003
(202) 547-7424

National Nursing League's Community Health Accreditation Program
350 Hudson St.
New York, NY 10014
(212) 989-2762
List of accredited agencies in your area.

HOSPICE

Foundation for Hospice and Homecare
(202) 547-7424
Educational materials; consumer guides.

HOUSING OPTIONS

American Association of Homes and Services for the Aging
(202) 783-2242
Brochures on how to choose an assisted-living facility and nursing home.

Assisted Living Federation of America
(703) 691-8100
Checklist for evaluating facilities.

National Citizen's Coalition for Nursing Home Reform
(202) 332-2275
Printed material.

INSURANCE

American Council of Life Insurance
(800) 338-4471
Brochure: "What You Should Know about Buying Life Insurance."

Health Insurance Association of America
(888) 844-2782
A free booklet, "Guide to Long-Term Care Insurance."

National Association of Insurance Commissioners
(816) 374-7259

A free brochure, "A Shopper's Guide to Long-Term Care Insurance."

Viatical Association of America
(800) 842-9811
Information about viatical settlements.

PENSIONS

Consumer Information Center
Dept. 521E
Pueblo, CO 81009
Booklet, "Your Guaranteed Pension," answers frequently asked questions about private pension plans.

RETIREMENT

National Center for Women and Retirement Research
(800) 426-7386
Printed material on saving for retirement.

SAVINGS

American Savings Education Council
(248) 775-6364; www.asec.org
Savings planning worksheet: "Ballpark Estimate."

National Association of Investors Corp.
(810) 583-6242; www.better-investing.org
Book (charge applies): *Starting and Running a Profitable Investment Club.*

SENIOR ASSOCIATIONS AND RESOURCES

American Association of Retired Persons
601 E St. NW
Washington, DC 20049
(202) 434-2277
Vast number of publications on elder and caregiver issues, from long-distance caregiving to reverse mortgages. The AARP prefers that you write to its fulfillment section for specific publications.

National Association for Hispanic Elderly
(212) 487-1922
Resources and publications in Spanish.

National Caucus and Center on Black Aged
(202) 637-8400
Variety of printed matter.

National Council on Aging
(202) 479-1200
Research reports, printed material.

National Hispanic Council on Aging
(202) 265-1288
Printed material.

STROKE

Courage Center
(615) 520-0520
Printed material for stroke victims and their families.

SERVICES

ALZHEIMER'S DISEASE

Family Relief Program of the Alzheimer's Association
(800) 437-2433
Emergency short-term day or respite care, nursing home
care, transportation, living expenses, and other expenses of
those with Alzheimer's disease.

CANCER

National Cancer Institute
(800) 422-6237
Hot line provides information on resources and referrals
for cancer patients.

CAREGIVING

National Alliance for Caregiving
(301) 718-8444
Resource center provides referrals, support.

CASE AND CARE MANAGEMENT

Aging Network Services
(301) 657-4329
Referrals for fee consultations.

National Association of Professional Geriatric Care
Managers
(520) 881-8008
Referrals to local members.

ELDERCARE LOCATOR

(800) 677-1116 (9 A.M. to 9 P.M. EST)
Government-funded hot line gives referrals to local eldercare agencies.

ELDER LAW

National Academy of Elder Law Attorneys
(520) 881-4005; www.naela.org.
Referral to an elder law attorney in your area.

GRIEF

Grief Recovery Institute
(800) 445-4808
Helpline, Monday through Friday, noon to 8 P.M.

HOUSING

National Council of Senior Citizens
(301) 578-8800
Referrals to long-term care services, nursing home alternatives.

U.S. Department of Housing and Urban Development
(HUD)
(800) 569-4287
Housing counselor.

INSURANCE

American Council of Life Insurance
(800) 338-4471
Offers the free brochure, "What You Should Know About
Buying Life Insurance."

National Insurance Consumer Helpline
(800) 942-4242
Answers questions about life, health, auto, and home insurance, Monday through Friday, 8 A.M. to 8 P.M. EST.

MORTGAGES

Federal National Mortgage Association (Fannie Mae)
(800) 732-6643
Referral to mortgage and reverse mortgage lenders in your
area.

ORGAN DONATIONS

United Network for Organ Sharing (UNOS)
(800) 24DONOR
Free organ donor card.

PENSIONS

Pension Rights Center
(202) 296-3776
Answers questions about pensions.

SENIORS ASSOCIATIONS

American Association of Retired Persons (AARP)
(800) 424-3410
Dues-collecting organization for those age 50 and over. Provides legal counsel, many other services for members.

National Hispanic Council on Aging
(202) 265-1288
Advocacy for Hispanic seniors, referrals to local agencies, resources.

Support Groups

Alzheimer's Association
(800) 272-3900
Referrals to local association support groups.

American Arthritis Association
(404) 872-7100
Referral to local association support groups.

American Cancer Society
(800) ACS-2345; www.cancer.org
Referral to local association support group.

American Lung Association
(800) LUNG-USA
www.lungusa.org

Leukemia Society of America
600 Third Ave.
New York, NY 10016
(800) 955-4LSA
www.leukemia.org

National Hospice Foundation
1901 N. Moore St. #901
Arlington, VA 22209
(703) 516-4928
Referral to local hospice grief support group.

National Marfan Foundation
382 Main St.
Port Washington, NY 11050
(800) 8MARFAN
www.marfan.org
Referrals to local support groups.

National Parkinson Foundation
(800) 327-4545; www.parkinson.org
Referral to local association support group.

National Stroke Network (American Heart Association)
(800) 553-6321

Trigeminal Neuralgia Association
P.O. Box 340
Barnegat Light, NJ 08006
(609) 361-1014
tna@lsionline.net
Referral to local support groups.

TRANSPORTATION

Angel Flight
(800) 352-4256 (24-hour hot line)
All-volunteer, nonprofit network of 630 pilots and 250 ground support personnel operating in Florida, Georgia, Alabama, Mississippi, and South Carolina. Flies sick and injured children and adults needing specialized medical care to hospitals. Pilots pay all costs.

PRODUCTS

ADVANCE DIRECTIVES

Choice in Dying
(800) 989-9455
Free living wills and state-specific medical power of attorney forms.

ALZHEIMER'S RELIEF

Alzheimer's Family Relief Program
(800) 437-2423
15825 Shady Grove Road, Suite 140
Rockville, MD 20850
Program of last resort. Provides for emergency short-term

nursing care, respite care or day care, and medications and medical supplies for people with Alzheimer's disease. Also pays for transportation and living expenses, personal hygiene supplies, and other expenses. You may apply for a grant of $500 every 90 days.

EYEGLASSES

Local chapters of Lions Clubs International provide refurbished eyeglasses to needy individuals.

HEARING AIDS

Hear Now
(800) 648-4327
New or near-new hearing aids for those unable to afford them. Call for information and application packet.

MEDICAL SUPPLIES AND EQUIPMENT

Arthritis Foundation
(800) 283-7800; www.arthritis.org
Local offices loan wheelchairs, canes, and crutches.

Family Relief Program of the Alzheimer's Association
(800) 437-2433
Emergency medication, medical supplies, personal hygiene supplies, and other items for loved ones with Alzheimer's disease.

PRESCRIPTION DRUGS

American Cancer Society
(800) ACS-2345; www.cancer.org
Local chapters have limited funds for emergency assistance to pay for drugs for cancer patients.

Family Relief Program of the Alzheimer's Association
(800) 437-2433
Emergency medication for loved ones with Alzheimer's disease.

Leukemia Society of America
600 Third Ave.
New York, NY 10016
(800) 955-4LSA
www.leukemia.org
Local chapters may provide up to $500 per fiscal year for drugs used in the treatment, care, and control of leukemia and allied diseases, dispensed through approved drug sources.

Pharmaceutical Research and Manufacturer's Association of America
(800) 762-4636
Receive prescription drugs from pharmaceutical companies at no cost (following eligibility guidelines).

Oxygen

American Lung Association
(800) LUNG-USA
Local chapters have limited funds to pay for emergency oxygen.